COLLINS

NATURE
QUIZ BOOK

HarperCollinsPublishers Ltd, 1995

77–85 Fulham Palace Road

London W6 8JB

Written by Michael Chinery

ISBN 0 00 220039 2

Printed in Great Britain by The Bath Press, Avon

Cover pictures courtesy of Tony Stone Images and Michael and Patricia Fogden

COLLINS

NATURE QUIZ BOOK

Michael Chinery

HarperCollins*Publishers*

Collins Nature Quiz Book has 100 quizzes and 100 tie-break questions for everyone interested in testing their knowledge of the natural world. Each quiz contains 20 questions of varying degrees of difficulty. Many of the answers give additional information, but as long as the key words are given in response, the answer may be accepted. In some cases, tricky words are spelt phonetically in order to minimise the risk of misunderstanding.

QUIZ 1

1 Which has the larger ears – the African or the Indian elephant?

2 How many petals does a poppy normally have?

3 Which is the largest of the apes?

4 What is the missing word: egg, ... , pupa, adult?

5 Man, fly and spider are all species of what kind of flower?

6 From which tree are cricket bats made?

7 In which country can you find wild koalas?

8 Apart from the bats, which are the only two British mammals that hibernate?

9 What do we call the process by which new plant and animal species develop from preexisting ones over a long period of time?

10 What is the defining characteristic of a deciduous tree?

11 What animal lives in a sett?

12 How many legs has a spider?

13 What does a palaeontologist (pal-ee-ont-ologist) study?

14 What is the main food of the giant panda?

15 Name Britain's only venomous snake

16 What do vertebrates have that invertebrates do not?

17 Which is the odd one out: ladybird, cockroach, cockchafer, weevil?

18 What is the world's largest living bird?

19 Who wrote the famous book *The Origin of Species*?

20 Peanuts grow on trees: true or false?

Answers 1

1 The African elephant

2 Four

3 The gorilla

4 Larva

5 Orchid

6 Willow

7 Australia

8 Dormouse and hedgehog

9 Evolution

10 It drops its leaves in the autumn

11 Badger

12 Eight

13 Fossils

14 Bamboo shoots and leaves

15 The adder or viper

16 A spine or backbone (accept vertebrae)

17 The cockroach: the others are all beetles

18 The ostrich

19 Charles Darwin

20 False: they grow on short plants that often sprawl over the ground. When the flowers have been pollinated, their stalks grow downwards and push the developing fruits into the soil – hence the alternative name of groundnuts

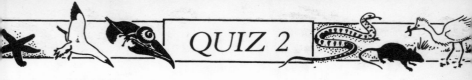

1 What is an earthstar?

2 What is the main food of a mole?

3 What is an hermaphrodite (her-maf-roe-dite) animal?

4 Name the famous series of natural history books, published by Collins, which first appeared in 1945 and now has over 80 titles

5 The salmon spends its early life in rivers and then goes down to the sea to breed: true or false?

6 How many wings does a house-fly have?

7 Name three 'royal' or 'aristocratic' butterflies that may be found in Britain

8 Approximately how old is the Earth: 10 million years, 250 million years, 1000 million years, or 4500 million years?

9 What common name is used to refer to trees such as cedars, larches, firs and pines?

10 The Greek philosopher Socrates (Sock-rat-ees) is reputed to have committed suicide by drinking an extract of which plant?

11 Did birds' wings evolve from the front legs or the back legs?

12 Does a grass snake lay eggs or give birth to active young?

13 What connects froghoppers, milkmaids and lords-and-ladies?

14 How many kinds of bee do we have in Great Britain: about 15, about 50, or about 250?

15 From what fruit do we obtain cider?

16 Where are the Royal Botanic Gardens?

17 What tree is famous for its large sticky buds?

18 Which bird walks under the water to collect its food?

19 To which order of mammals do the porcupines belong?

20 What is the Long Man of Wilmington?

Answers 2

1 A fungus, related to the puffballs and named because its outer coat peels back to form a star-like base

2 Earthworms

3 An animal with both male and female organs in the same individual. Earthworms and garden snails are familiar examples

4 The New Naturalist series

5 False: the salmon breeds in the rivers. The young fish swim down to the sea and return to the rivers to spawn when they are mature

6 Two

7 Purple emperor, Duke of Burgundy, Queen of Spain fritillary, or monarch. The first two are resident in Britain and the other two are rare visitors

8 4500 million years

9 Conifers, because they all carry their seeds in cones

10 Hemlock

11 The front legs

12 It lays eggs

13 Cuckoo: froghopper nymphs make the frothy 'cuckoo-spit' found on plants in the spring; milkmaids is another name for the cuckooflower; cuckoopint is another name for lords-and-ladies

14 About 250 kinds of bee

15 Apples

16 At Kew, just to the west of London and in Edinburgh

17 Horse chestnut

18 Dipper

19 The Rodentia or rodents

20 A large figure of a man, cut into the chalk downs in Sussex

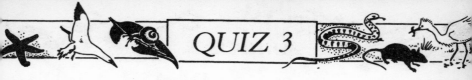

QUIZ 3

1 What is the world's largest fish?

2 Where did the dodo live?

3 Which British mammal has a brush?

4 What birds belong to the order Strigiformes (Stridge-ee-form-ees)?

5 Name the long-distance footpath that runs for 85 miles from Ivinghoe Beacon in the Chilterns to Avebury in Wiltshire

6 What does a fungicide do?

7 What parts of a flower produce the pollen?

8 What is the name of Britain's legless lizard?

9 Skippers, morphos and hairstreaks are members of which large group of insects?

10 What is the common English name of the flowers whose scientific name is *Myosotis*?

11 Where does the kingfisher make its nest?

12 To which plant family do the cereals belong?

13 The Norfolk Broads are man-made: true or false?

14 What is botany?

15 Where would you expect to find a bracket fungus?

16 What kind of insect is an old lady?

17 What period in the earth's history came between the Permian and Jurassic periods?

18 What do we call an adult male seal?

19 What do broomrape, dodder and toothwort have in common?

20 Do spruce cones hang from the branches or stand erect?

1 The whale shark. It can exceed 15 metres in length and weigh over 40 tonnes

2 The island of Mauritius in the Indian Ocean

3 The fox

4 Owls

5 The Ridgeway Path

6 It kills fungi

7 The anthers, which are little pouches at the tips of the stamens

8 The slow-worm

9 Butterflies

10 Forget-me-nots

11 In a tunnel or burrow in a river bank

12 The grass family or Poaceae (accept Gramineae, which is the old name for the family)

13 True: they are old peat-pits which have since become flooded. The peat was dug for fuel for several hundred years, but digging stopped in the 13th century – probably because a rise in sea level initiated flooding

14 The study of plants or plant life

15 Growing on a tree trunk or a log

16 A moth

17 The Triassic Period

18 A bull

19 They are all parasitic plants with no chlorophyll. They 'steal' their food by sending suckers into other plants

20 They hang down

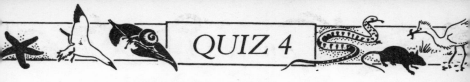

QUIZ 4

1 What are spleenworts and polypodies?

2 What do we call a female red deer?

3 Which butterfly is the odd one out: green-veined white, large white, marbled white, wood white?

4 The kiwi lays the largest egg of any bird: true or false?

5 What connects the dunnock or hedge sparrow and the plant known as selfheal?

6 Name the large, aquatic South American rodent, introduced to Britain for fur-farming in the 1930s, that became a serious pest in East Anglia

7 What do we call the larva of a crane-fly?

8 Name the monk who began the study of genetics by studying garden peas

9 Which was Britain's first National Park?

10 Would you find penguins in the Arctic Ocean or the Antarctic Ocean?

11 What is the more common name of the tree known as gean?

12 Where would you have to go in order to watch lemurs in the wild?

13 How did the bird's nest orchid get its name?

14 What is the food-plant of the caterpillar of the cinnabar moth?

15 What do the initials RSPB stand for?

16 What rodents are said to commit suicide by rushing into rivers and drowning?

17 What name is sometimes given to a flock of goldfinches?

18 What name is given to the resting place of a hare?

19 Which Scottish loch is reputed to hold a monster?

20 What is a mermaid's purse?

1 They are kinds of ferns

2 A hind

3 The marbled white: it belongs to the 'brown' family or Satyridae, while the others are true whites belonging to the Pieridae

4 False: the ostrich lays the largest egg of any bird, but the kiwi lays the largest egg in relation to its body weight – the egg weighs about a quarter as much as the bird itself

5 Both have the generic name *Prunella*. The dunnock is *Prunella modularis* and the selfheal is *Prunella vulgaris*

6 The coypu, whose fur is called nutria

7 A leatherjacket

8 Gregor Mendel

9 The Peak District National Park, first designated in December 1950

10 The Antarctic

11 The wild cherry

12 The island of Madagascar: this is the only place where these monkey-like animals still exist

13 Because its roots form a tangled cluster looking vaguely like a bird's nest

14 Ragwort. The black and yellow caterpillars have actually been used to control this poisonous weed on grazing land

15 The Royal Society for the Protection of Birds

16 Lemmings, but the animals are not intentionally committing suicide: from time to time their populations build up to enormous numbers and the animals get the urge to emigrate and find new homes. They stream out in all directions and many die as they try to swim across rivers or even the sea

17 A charm

18 A form

19 Loch Ness

20 The horny egg-case of a dogfish, skate, or other shark-like fish

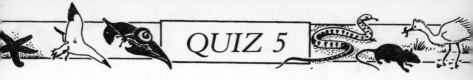

QUIZ 5

1 What sort of animals belong to the family Ursidae?

2 *Convallaria majalis* is the national flower of Sweden. By what common name do we know it in Britain?

3 Centipede, crab, spider, woodlouse. Only one of these animals is an arachnid: which one is it?

4 What gives the wings of butterflies and moths their colourful patterns?

5 What are bongos, kudus (koo–doos) and duikers (dye-kers)?

6 What are nidifugous (nid-ee-few-gus) birds?

7 Name the process by which green plants harness the energy of sunlight to make their food

8 Which part of the rhubarb plant do we eat?

9 What name is given to a male falcon?

10 Jane Goodall wrote a famous book called *In the Shadow of Man*, in which she described her work with which animals?

11 Where do benthic animals live?

12 What were *Eohippus* and *Merychippus*?

13 What do we call the fruit of the oak tree?

14 Bulbous, meadow and creeping are species of what kind of flower?

15 Only one bird belonging to the order Apodiformes (Ay-poe-dee-form-ees) is regularly found in the British Isles. What is its name?

16 Which is the odd one out: sperm whale, sei whale, minke whale, humpback whale?

17 What kind of insect is a devil's coachhorse?

18 What is the name for a group of lions?

19 The sardine is a young pilchard: true or false?

20 What is a prehensile tail?

1 Bears

2 Lily of the valley

3 The spider: the centipede belongs to the group known as chilopods, while the crab and the woodlouse are crustaceans

4 Minute scales that coat the wings like miniature roof-tiles and rub off very easily if the wings are touched

5 They are kinds of antelope

6 Birds that leave the nest soon after hatching – from the Latin words *nidus*, meaning a nest, and *fugere*, meaning to flee. They include many water birds and ground-nesting species

7 Photosynthesis

8 The leaf stalk or petiole

9 Tercel or Tiercel

10 Chimpanzees

11 On the sea bed or on the bed of a river or lake

12 Extinct ancestors of the horse

13 An acorn

14 Buttercups

15 The swift

16 The sperm whale: it is a toothed whale and the others are all whale-bone whales that filter their food from the water

17 A beetle: it belongs to the group known as rove beetles, which have very short wing cases. It is also called a cock-tail beetle, because it raises its rear end when disturbed

18 A pride

19 True

20 A tail that can grip branches like an extra hand

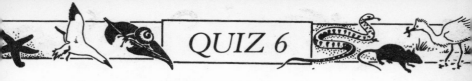

QUIZ 6

1 What are dholes, dingoes and zorros?

2 What does a dendrologist study?

3 What is wrong with the following observation? 'We all had our binoculars trained on the kiwis as they picked their way through the forest at nightfall, but a shot rang out and the birds immediately flew high into the trees.'

4 What insects belong to the order Trichoptera?

5 Which is the heaviest British bird?

6 Where does the caterpillar of the large blue butterfly spend most of its life?

7 Where would you expect to find a jew's ear fungus growing?

8 To what group of animals does the word caprine refer?

9 From what kind of flower do we get the expensive spice called saffron?

10 What animal lives in a holt?

11 Which mammal comes first in any alphabetical list of animals?

12 What name is given to a young grasshopper or any other young insect that looks quite like the adult and does not go through a chrysalis stage in its life history?

13 What is the common name of the insect whose scientific name is *Pulex irritans*?

14 Which is the odd one out: cod, haddock, whiting, plaice?

15 What is the emblem of the National Trust?

16 Who presented the television series *Life on Earth*?

17 What are osiers used for?

18 What is the largest living thing in the world?

19 What is the main food of the crossbill?

20 The death's head hawkmoth sometimes enters beehives to drink honey: true or false?

1 Wild dogs. The dhole lives in India, the dingo in Australia, and the zorro in South America

2 Trees

3 Kiwis cannot fly!

4 Caddis flies

5 The mute swan, which can weigh up to 20 kg

6 In an ant nest. Ants seek out young caterpillars and carry them into the nests, where the caterpillars feed on the ant grubs. In return, they give out a sugary secretion that the ants love to drink

7 On tree trunks and branches, especially on elder trees

8 Goats

9 From crocuses, mainly the Mediterranean *Crocus sativus*. The dried styles and stigmas are used to flavour and colour food, and the spice is very expensive because each flower has just one branching style and collecting them is hard work

10 An otter

11 The aardvark

12 A nymph

13 The human flea

14 The plaice: it is a flatfish

15 A sprig of oak leaves

16 David Attenborough

17 For basket-making: they are small willows with pliable young twigs

18 One of the giant sequoia or wellingtonia trees: some of these trees are nearly 90 m (300 ft) high and weigh over 2000 tonnes – as much as 20 good-sized blue whales!

19 The seeds of spruces and other conifers. The bird uses the crossed tips of its beak to lever up the cone scales and expose the seeds

20 True

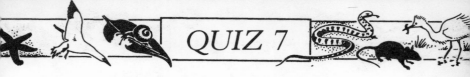

QUIZ 7

1 From what kind of plant do we get vanilla?

2 What do we call a young hare?

3 What tree has varieties called black, white and Lombardy?

4 The snow leopard lives only in the Rocky Mountains of North America: true or false?

5 Name two thrushes that regularly visit the British Isles for the winter

6 What does a hermit crab use for a home?

7 What sort of plant is a moonwort?

8 What colour is a chanterelle?

9 Name the order to which butterflies and moths belong

10 What animals go about in mobs?

11 What crop is attacked by the Colorado beetle?

12 On an Ordnance Survey map, what is represented by a red or pink triangle?

13 Who founded the Wildfowl and Wetlands Trust?

14 How did bird's-foot trefoil get its name?

15 The nectarine is a variety of which popular fruit?

16 How many horns does the Indian rhino have?

17 What colour is chlorophyll?

18 What are the sickener, the blusher and the deceiver?

19 Which London park would you be in if you were at London Zoo?

20 The grey squirrel is not native in the British Isles. Where did it come from?

1 An orchid

2 A leveret

3 Poplar

4 False: it lives only in the mountains of Asia

5 Redwing and fieldfare

6 The empty shell of a sea snail

7 A small fern

8 Yellow or pale orange: it is a fungus

9 Lepidoptera

10 Kangaroos

11 Potatoes

12 A youth hostel

13 Sir Peter Scott

14 Because its seed pods fan out like the toes of a bird

15 The peach

16 One

17 Green

18 Fungi or toadstools

19 Regent's Park

20 North America

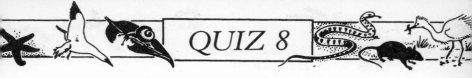

QUIZ 8

1 By what name do we know the female fox?

2 Who wrote *Silent Spring* – a book drawing attention to the problems of pesticides and how they can get into the food chains and poison birds and the whole environment?

3 What, in the world of moths, may be red, yellow, copper, or straw?

4 Why does the sundew have sticky leaves?

5 *Oryx* is the journal of which international conservation organisation?

6 Name two European birds whose names suggest towns or regions in the British Isles

7 What is honeydew?

8 What colour is wild cherry blossom?

9 What do the initials RSNC mean to a nature lover?

10 We have three native coniferous trees: yew is one, what are the other two?

11 What animals make up the class of molluscs known as gastropods?

12 What is a panther?

13 The male stickleback builds a nest and then persuades a female to lay her eggs in it: true or false?

14 What colour is a fly agaric?

15 How many points must a red deer stag have on its antlers before it can be called a royal?

16 What is a laughing jackass?

17 Where can you visit the Princess of Wales Conservatory?

18 The crab-eater seal is poorly named. What does it eat?

19 How many of the following are insects: scorpion, centipede, water flea, shrimp?

20 From which fish do we obtain caviar?

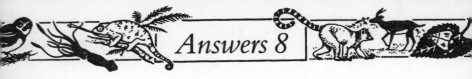

Answers 8

1 A vixen

2 Rachel Carson. Publication of this book in 1962 marked the birth of the modern environmental movement

3 Underwings

4 To trap small insects, which it then digests

5 Fauna and Flora International (formerly The Fauna and Flora Preservation Society)

6 Any two of the following: Dartford warbler, Kentish plover, Sandwich tern, Manx shearwater, Brent goose, Barrow's goldeneye

7 The sugary liquid exuded by aphids and some other plant-feeding bugs: when feeding on sap, they take in far more sugar than they need and simply pump the excess material out at the other end

8 White

9 The Royal Society for Nature Conservation

10 Scots pine and juniper

11 Slugs and snails

12 A leopard (or a jaguar) with a black coat. Also a name for puma in USA

13 True

14 Red and white

15 12, with at least 6 on each antler: the 3 topmost points or tines form an open cup rather like a crown

16 The kookaburra, which is a large Australian kingfisher: it is also called the alarm bird or breakfast bird because it starts its loud, chuckling call at about breakfast time

17 Kew Gardens

18 It eats krill and other small floating animals or plankton, which it strains from the water with its comb-like teeth

19 None of these is an insect!

20 The sturgeon

QUIZ 9

1 What do we call the fruits of the blackthorn?

2 What is the calyx of a flower?

3 What sort of animal is a treecreeper?

4 Name the disease that almost wiped out the British rabbit population during the 1950s

5 Name the tough grass that is widely planted to stabilise coastal sand dunes

6 What domesticated animal is affected by Isle of Wight disease?

7 Apart from the fact that they fly by day, what is unusual about bee hawkmoths?

8 What name is given to a male swan?

9 Name the two seals that regularly breed around the British coasts

10 Who wrote The *Naked Ape*?

11 What does an entomologist study?

12 Which is the only species of deer in which the female has antlers?

13 Which is the odd one out: spider monkey, squirrel monkey, howler monkey, rhesus monkey?

14 What name is commonly given to a group of wolves?

15 What tree has the scientific name *Fagus sylvatica*?

16 How does the coat of a jaguar differ from that of a leopard?

17 How did the flower ragged robin get its name?

18 What name is given to a young horse or zebra?

19 The word glabrous often appears in the descriptions of plants and insects. What does it mean?

20 What is wrong with the following diary entry? 'We set out to shake down our Christmas dinner with a walk over the Breckland. Snow had been falling in the morning and we could see the tracks of many birds. On following one set of tracks, we came upon a small group of stone curlews furiously scraping away the snow as they searched for insects on the ground.'

1 Sloes

2 The cluster of sepals at the base of the flower

3 A small bird, named for its habit of creeping up tree trunks and searching for insects in the bark crevices

4 Myxomatosis

5 Marram grass

6 The honey bee

7 Nearly all their scales are missing. Most of the scales fall during the moths' first flight, leaving the wings transparent like those of bees

8 A cob

9 The common or harbour seal and the grey seal

10 Desmond Morris: it is a book about human behaviour, showing that man is still very much like the apes in many ways

11 Insects

12 The reindeer

13 The rhesus monkey: it lives in Asia, but the others are all South American monkeys

14 A pack

15 The beech

16 Both these cats have spotted coats, with many of the spots arranged in rings or rosettes, but the rosettes of the jaguar each have a central spot

17 Because the petals are all deeply split and appear ragged

18 A foal

19 Smooth or hairless

20 Stone curlews are summer visitors to Britain

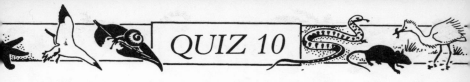

QUIZ 10

1 Which member of the cat family is often known as the hunting leopard?

2 To which family of plants does the cyclamen belong?

3 Which group of moths contains species called early, August and September?

4 What is a wobbegong?

5 What sort of food does a phytophagous animal eat?

6 In which area of London is the Natural History Museum?

7 What colour is a hooded crow?

8 Name the largest of the whales (also the largest of all living animals)

9 What do we call the milky juice that flows from broken dandelion stems and various other plants, including the rubber tree?

10 What is the collective name for a group of peacocks?

11 Which bird's call is likened to 'a little bit of bread and no cheese'?

12 Name the long-distance footpath that runs from Derbyshire to the Scottish border

13 The fly orchid is pollinated by flies: true or false?

14 What colour is the pasque flower?

15 Apart from their size, how can you tell a stoat from a weasel?

16 In the living world, what are smuts and rusts?

17 What group of animals includes species called the banded wedge, the warty venus and the cross-cut carpet?

18 What do we call the fruits of the wild rose?

19 Which insects transmit malaria?

20 What is the scientific name of the human species?

1 The cheetah

2 The primrose family or Primulaceae

3 The thorn moths

4 An Australian shark

5 Plants

6 South Kensington

7 Black and grey

8 The blue whale, which can reach over 30 m (100 ft) in length and weigh up to 147 tonnes (150 tons)

9 Latex

10 A muster

11 The yellowhammer

12 The Pennine Way

13 False: it is pollinated by small wasps, although flies and other insects may visit it occasionally

14 Violet or purple

15 The stoat always has a black tip to its tail

16 They are fungi causing diseases of cereals and many other plants

17 Bivalve molluscs (accept sea shells)

18 Hips

19 Mosquitoes

20 *Homo sapiens*

QUIZ 11

1 Which animal is sometimes known as the old man of the woods?

2 Which bird has the most feathers?

3 What is the proper name for a butterfly's tongue?

4 To what season does the adjective vernal apply?

5 To what family does the budgerigar belong?

6 What is a halophyte?

7 Why do some holly trees never bear berries?

8 What does it mean if an insect is described as alate?

9 From what is laver bread made?

10 Which two continents are the native home of the cacti?

11 The eyes of a plaice are on the left side of its head: true or false?

12 Why is the bird's-nest fungus so called?

13 When did the Cambrian Period begin: about 6 million years ago, about 60 million years ago, or about 600 million years ago?

14 What is the main food of the osprey?

15 What animals can be ringed, bearded, or hooded?

16 *Armeria maritima* turns many of our cliffs pink in the summer. What is its common name?

17 What was the nationality of Linnaeus, who laid the foundations of the modern system for classifying plants and animals?

18 A flock of what kind of birds is sometimes called an unkindness?

19 What is herpetology?

20 What colour is the dye obtained from the woad plant?

1 The orang-utan

2 The swan: 25,216 feathers were once counted on a North American whistling swan

3 The proboscis

4 Spring

5 The parrot family or Psittacidae

6 Any salt-tolerant plant, such as you might find growing on or near the seashore

7 Because holly trees are either male or female and only female trees have berries

8 It has wings

9 A red seaweed, especially from species of *Porphyra*

10 North America and South America, with most species coming from the deserts of North and Central America

11 False: the adult plaice lies on its left side and both eyes come to lie on the right side of the head, looking up into the water

12 Because its spores are borne in egg-like packets that sit in nest-like cups

13 About 600 million years ago

14 Fish

15 Seals

16 Thrift

17 Swedish

18 Ravens, although the word is now rarely used in this way

19 The study of reptiles and amphibians

20 Blue

QUIZ 12

1. What is a saguaro?

2. Where in England is the Breckland?

3. What kinds of insects belong to the order Orthoptera?

4. What is the more common name of the windhover?

5. What is ophiophobia (off-ee-o-foe-bee-a)?

6. In America, this butterfly is called the mourning cloak. What do we call it in Britain?

7. To which animals does the word lupine refer?

8. The Great Barrier Reef lies off the coast of which country?

9. What is the main cause of hay fever?

10. What name is given to a baby elephant?

11. Which American bird got its name from its habit of running alongside stage coaches and snapping up the insects and other animals disturbed by the horses and the wheels?

12. Name the world's largest deer

13. What rock forms most of the Chiltern Hills and the White Cliffs of Dover?

14. Which part of the hop plant is used in brewing beer?

15. What do we call animals that have no dark pigments in their skins and are therefore completely white?

16. What do vampire bats eat?

17. What bird is featured on the logo of the RSPB?

18. What are Tamworths, saddlebacks and large whites?

19. What is a glis-glis?

20. Where does the cuckoo build its nest?

1 A large, tree-like cactus growing in the deserts of North America

2 On the borders of Norfolk and Suffolk: it is a sandy region supporting many plants that otherwise grow only near the coast

3 Grasshoppers and crickets

4 The kestrel

5 The fear of snakes

6 The Camberwell Beauty

7 Wolves

8 Australia – off the coast of Queensland

9 Grass pollen drifting in the air. The pollens of some other plants, including stinging nettles and plantains, may also be involved

10 A calf

11 The roadrunner

12 The moose or elk, which stands up to 2.2 m (7 ft 3 in) at the shoulder and weighs up to 1760 lb (800 kg). It lives in the northern forests and is called the moose in North America and the elk in Europe

13 Chalk

14 The female flower cluster, also called the cone

15 Albinos

16 Blood

17 The avocet

18 Breeds of pig

19 A large dormouse. It is often called the edible dormouse because it was regarded as a delicacy by the Romans. It was introduced to Britain from the continent in 1902

20 Cuckoos do not build nests: female cuckoos lay their eggs in the nests of other birds

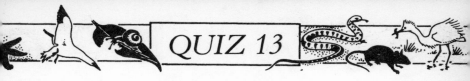

QUIZ 13

1 What is the common name of *Musca domestica*?

2 What is a ptarmigan (tar-mig-an)?

3 In which country is the Gran Paradiso National Park?

4 Which flower is the national emblem of India?

5 What are Bartlett, comice and conference?

6 Camel-hair paint brushes are made from real camel hair: true or false?

7 When do diurnal animals sleep?

8 Who made his dogs drool by ringing bells?

9 Which British butterfly is found only on the Isle of Wight?

10 What do we call an adult male badger?

11 Where would you go to see wild wombats?

12 What is palynology (pal-in-ology)?

13 What do the initials BTO stand for?

14 Name the largest European rodent

15 Pine needles always grow in clusters: are those of the Scots pine in twos, threes, or fives?

16 What colour are the flowers of creeping jenny?

17 Name the three parts into which an insect's body is divided

18 How many eyes does a bat have?

19 What would you do with the leaves of *Camellia sinensis*?

20 The garden polyanthus has been developed from a hybrid between a primrose and which other flower?

1 The house-fly

2 A game bird belonging to the grouse family

3 Italy

4 The sacred lotus

5 Varieties of pears

6 False: they are made from the fine hairs from squirrels' tails and got their name from a Mr Camel who first produced them

7 At night: diurnal means that they are active by day

8 Ivan Pavlov, a Russian biologist who rang bells every time he fed his dogs. The animals quickly learned to associate the bells with food and began to salivate as soon as they heard them ringing

9 The Glanville Fritillary

10 A boar

11 Australia: they are large, burrowing marsupials

12 The study of pollen grains

13 British Trust for Ornithology

14 The beaver

15 In twos

16 Yellow

17 Head, thorax and abdomen

18 Two, just like any other mammal

19 Put them in a tea-pot and make a cup of tea

20 The cowslip

QUIZ 14

1 Who was the zoo keeper in TV's *Animal Magic*?

2 What animal has the scientific name *Ursus maritimus*?

3 In which country is the Cevennes National Park?

4 What make up the bulk of the pangolin's diet?

5 In which month does the hawthorn traditionally bloom?

6 The bald eagle is the national emblem of the USA, but is it really bald?

7 What do the initials FSC mean to a naturalist?

8 What kinds of insects belong to the order Hymenoptera?

9 Name Britain's largest native, land-living carnivorous mammal

10 Where do pelagic animals live?

11 What do edentate mammals not have?

12 What is a bobolink?

13 What can be crack, white, or weeping?

14 What name is commonly given to a female donkey?

15 All ivory comes from elephants: true or false?

16 What common plants belong to the genus *Veronica*?

17 Where would you be most likely to find springtails?

18 What is the name of the sensitive line on each side of a fish that detects movement and changes of pressure in the surrounding water?

19 Why might a naturalist be interested in a pluviometer?

20 How many spices are there in a jar of Allspice?

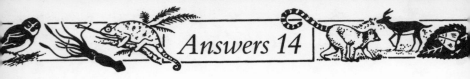

Answers 14

1 Johnny Morris

2 The polar bear

3 France

4 Ants and termites: pangolins are often called scaly anteaters

5 May: the flowers are often called may-blossom

6 No: it merely looks bald from a distance because of the white feathers on its head and neck

7 Field Studies Council – an organisation involved with the teaching of environmental studies, especially at its Field Centres scattered around the country

8 Bees, wasps, ants, sawflies and ichneumons are the main insects belonging to this order

9 The badger. The fox may be taller, but is much slimmer and weighs much less

10 The open sea, especially in the surface layers

11 Teeth

12 A bird: it is a small American songbird, whose song sounds a bit like *bob-o-link, bob-o-link*

13 Willow trees

14 A jenny

15 False: the tusks of walruses and narwhals are also made of ivory

16 Speedwells

17 In leaf litter or soil: they are tiny insect-like creatures that feed mainly on decaying leaves

18 The lateral line

19 Because it is another name for a rain gauge, measuring the amount of rainfall

20 One: allspice is the name of one particular spice that gets its name because it combines the flavours of several other spices

QUIZ 15

1 What do wireworms become when they grow up?

2 What bird was once called the laverock, especially in Scotland and northern England?

3 What kind of insect is a firefly?

4 What would you be eating if you had a dish of Cambridge Rivals in front of you?

5 Name the first dog in space

6 What is permafrost?

7 In the plant kingdom, what is the fundamental difference between a horsetail and a mare's-tail?

8 Which group of butterflies have species called Essex, dingy and silver-spotted?

9 What name is sometimes given to a flock of starlings?

10 What is the collective name for all the animal life of a region?

11 Medieval archers used chestnut wood for their long-bows: true or false?

12 Where would you go to look for whirligig beetles?

13 What is a stinkhorn?

14 In America it is called the common gallinule. What do we call this bird in Britain?

15 What is the Westbury White Horse if it is not a pub?

16 What do the letters AONB mean in the context of the countryside?

17 What animal traditionally goes mad in March?

18 What makes a jumping bean jump?

19 What do we call the phenomenon by which a harmless or defenceless creature gains protection by resembling something poisonous or otherwise unpleasant?

20 Name the famous French naturalist often referred to as 'The Insect Man'

1 Click beetles

2 The skylark

3 A beetle

4 Strawberries

5 Laika

6 The permanently frozen ground of the polar regions

7 The horsetail is a flowerless plant, related to the ferns and reproducing by scattering spores, but the mare's-tail is a flowering plant that produces seeds

8 The skippers

9 A murmuration

10 Fauna

11 False: they used yew wood

12 Ponds and other still or slow-moving fresh water: the beetles got their name for their habit of zooming round and round on the surface

13 A fungus with an appalling smell

14 The moorhen

15 A large figure of a horse cut in the chalk downs above Westbury in Wiltshire

16 Area of Outstanding Natural Beauty

17 The hare

18 A small insect grub inside the seed: if it gets too hot in the sun, the grub wriggles violently and makes the seed jump, and if it is lucky it will eventually end up in the shade

19 Mimicry

20 Henri Fabre

QUIZ 16

1 Ladybirds get more spots as they grow older: true or false?

2 What is the more common name of the golden-rain tree, a common garden tree with poisonous seeds?

3 What are meanders?

4 Which is the odd one out: wheatear, corncrake, corn bunting?

5 Where did Lord Rothschild set up his famous natural history collection, which now forms part of the Natural History Museum?

6 In what kind of habitat would you be most likely to find Apollo butterflies?

7 What name is normally given to an adult male fox?

8 What is oology (oh-ology)?

9 Who might use a mercury vapour trap?

10 A crocus grows from a bulb: true or false?

11 Why is the spitting spider so called?

12 Which botanist went on a TV safari in his back yard?

13 What do the following have in common: ash, avens, pansy, ringlet?

14 What is wrong with the following diary entry? 'We watched the jaguar inch slowly towards the antelope, and then, just as it prepared to pounce, the antelope was grabbed by a huge anaconda.'

15 Name the zoo perched high on the downs near Dunstable

16 What nickname is often given to the wren?

17 What is the food-plant of the caterpillar of the peacock butterfly?

18 A ferret is a domesticated form of which animal?

19 What is the alternative name of bittersweet?

20 What do we call insects whose young grubs or larvae tunnel between the upper and lower surfaces of leaves?

1 False: once ladybirds get their wings and spotted wing-cases they are fully grown and do not change thereafter

2 Laburnum

3 Wide, sweeping bends in a river

4 Corn bunting: it lives in Britain all the year, but the others are summer visitors

5 Tring in Hertfordshire

6 Mountains in many parts of the world, but not in Britain

7 A dog

8 The study of eggs

9 Moth hunters: moths are drawn to mercury vapour lamps form long distances

10 False: crocuses grow from corms

11 Because it spits poisonous gum at its prey, paralysing it and fixing it down at the same time

12 David Bellamy

13 Each can be preceded by mountain to form the name of another plant or animal

14 Jaguars and anacondas live in South America, but antelopes live in Africa and Asia

15 Whipsnade

16 Jenny

17 Stinging nettle

18 The polecat

19 Woody nightshade

20 Leaf miners

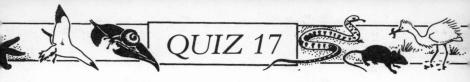

QUIZ 17

1 What colour are the flowers of the horse chestnut tree?

2 What are the smallest of all flowering plants?

3 Which is the odd one out: grass snake, smooth snake, whip snake, asp?

4 What is unusual about Manx cats?

5 A popular song once told us that 'there's an awful lot of coffee in Brazil', but where did coffee originally come from?

6 What kinds of insects live in apiaries?

7 What is the common name of the animal scientifically known as *Mus musculus*?

8 How many teeth does the blue whale have?

9 What is wrong with the following diary entry? 'We had landed on a remote, uninhabited island in the hope of finding some giant tortoises. We saw no sign of them for several hours, but then, under a large tree, we found some large fallen fruits with the unmistakable imprints of the tortoises' teeth. We knew we were getting close.'

10 What colour are owls' eggs?

11 Which common garden shrub contains cyanide in its leaves?

12 Name the world's largest lizard

13 What would you do with a root of *Pastinaca sativa*?

14 What is an aye-aye?

15 When are crepuscular creatures on the move?

16 Rivers are divided into several reaches, each with its own kinds of fish and other animals. What do we call the uppermost reach of a river?

17 What trees can be maritime, umbrella and lodgepole?

18 In which English county is the famous bird reserve of Minsmere?

19 What is the national flower of Wales?

20 What name is given to the hairy caterpillars of tiger moths and also to the larvae of carpet beetles?

1 White or cream

2 The floating duckweeds, especially one called *Wolffia* which is no more than a millimetre across

3 The asp: it is the only venomous snake of the four

4 They have no tails

5 Africa, especially from Ethiopia

6 Honey bees

7 The house mouse

8 None: it is one of the baleen whales that feed on small planktonic animals strained from the water with 'curtains' of whalebone or baleen hanging from the jaws

9 Tortoises have no teeth: they bite their food with very hard, horny beak

10 White – in common with most eggs that are laid in dark holes

11 The cherry laurel, often simply called laurel

12 The Komodo dragon, which lives on the Indonesian island of Komodo

13 Cook it and eat it: it is a parsnip

14 A very rare lemur – a distant relative of the monkeys

15 At dusk or just before dawn, in the twilight

16 The headstream

17 Pines

18 Suffolk

19 The daffodil

20 Woolly bears

1 What is an arboretum?

2 Which snake has the longest fangs?

3 Which is the odd one out: beaver, mink, marmot, woodchuck?

4 In which country is The Burren, a botanically rich area of limestone?

5 What is the more popular or familiar name of the antirrhinum?

6 What important anti-malarial drug and drink-flavouring do we obtain from the cinchona (sin-cone-a) tree?

7 Which butterfly, a rare visitor to Britain, is named after an area of London?

8 What kinds of animals belong to the family Ranidae?

9 What is a saprophyte?

10 At what time of year does the hazel come into flower?

11 What do cotton grass, grass of Parnassus and scurvygrass all have in common?

12 What kind of cat is a caracal?

13 What colour is a live lobster?

14 A lichen is a combination of a fungus with what other kind of organism?

15 Piltdown Man was a direct ancestor of the human race: true or false?

16 Why are compass termites so called?

17 Which species of kite breeds in Britain?

18 Where is the original home of the Colorado beetle?

19 What is the main food of the wombat?

20 Where would you look for devil's toenails?

1 A collection of living trees or tree garden

2 The Gaboon viper: its fangs are up to 5 cm (2 in) long

3 The mink: it is a carnivore and the others are rodents

4 Eire or Ireland

5 Snapdragon

6 Quinine

7 Camberwell Beauty

8 Frogs

9 A plant that obtains its food from dead and decaying matter, such as rotting wood. Many fungi are also saprophytes

10 Early spring

11 None of them is a true grass

12 A lynx, although it is probably only distantly related to the other lynxes

13 Dark blue or black: it turns red only when cooked

14 An alga

15 False: Piltdown man was a hoax. The bones dug up near Piltdown in Sussex were originally thought to belong to an early member of the human race, but were later proved to be a mixture of modern human and ape bones

16 Because these Australian termites build their wall-like nests in a north–south direction. This allows the nests to warm up quickly in the morning but does not expose too much surface to the mid-day sun

17 The red kite

18 North America

19 Grass

20 In rocks, cliffs or quarries: they are fossil shells shaped rather like large toenails

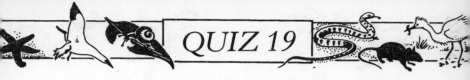

QUIZ 19

1 What are you likely to be doing if you are staying at Juniper Hall, Flatford Mill, or Preston Montford?

2 What is the chemical name of the main component of marsh gas?

3 Are the stems of sedges square, triangular, or round in cross section?

4 What kind of animal is a sea mouse?

5 Why might a hunter search for slots in the ground?

6 What do we call the process by which an area of land is colonised by a sequence of plants and gradually converted to woodland?

7 What name is given to the home of a colony of rabbits?

8 What common trees belong to the genus *Quercus*?

9 When was the last wild wolf seen in Britain: in the 1740s, the 1840s, or the 1890s?

10 Where would you find glasswort growing in the wild?

11 What is proper name for the stalk of a leaf?

12 What is the title of the national magazine of the Wildlife Trusts?

13 What colour is the tail of a redstart?

14 How would you know that you were approaching a colony of the plant known as ramsons?

15 Name the two species of rat living wild in Britain

16 What are pteridophytes (terrid-oh-fites)?

17 What do we call the offspring of male horse and female donkey?

18 What is entomophobia (ento-mow-foe-bee-a)?

19 What animals is the mongoose traditionally used to control?

20 The guillemot lays its single egg on a bare rock ledge. Why does the egg not roll off?

1 Attending a field course: these are three of the Field Centres run by the Field Studies Council to promote understanding and awareness of the countryside and environment

2 Methane

3 Triangular: a useful memory aid is 'sedges have edges'

4 A worm: it is one of the bristleworms, but the bristles are so long and dense that they look like fur

5 Because slots is another name for footprints, especially of deer

6 Succession

7 A warren

8 Oaks

9 1740s

10 On muddy seashores and estuaries

11 The petiole

12 Natural World

13 Red: 'start' in this context is derived from the Old English word *steort* meaning tail

14 It smells strongly of garlic

15 The black rat and brown rat

16 Ferns and their relatives (accept club–mosses and horsetails)

17 A hinny

18 The fear of insects

19 Snakes

20 Because the egg is pointed at one end and if disturbed it just rolls round in a circle

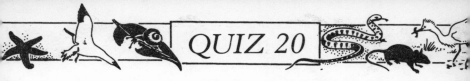

QUIZ 20

1 What is the largest wild member of the dog family?

2 In which country is Europe's largest glacier?

3 What is the normal human body temperature in degrees centigrade?

4 Name the organisation that owns about one sixth of the entire British coastline – over 500 miles in total

5 Name the insect that produces cuckoo-spit on plants in the spring

6 What colour is a male brimstone butterfly?

7 What is a marsupium?

8 Which is the odd one out: box, hazel, dogwood, spindle?

9 How often does the seashore experience spring tides?

10 What common bird has the scientific name *Troglodytes troglodytes*?

11 What shape are reniform leaves?

12 What do we call the technique of growing miniature trees in pots?

13 What is the difference between an ibex and an ibis?

14 What do we call the little flowers that make up the flower heads of daisies and dandelions?

15 What is a whale's blowhole?

16 Who wrote the book *Food for Free*, describing how you can obtain food from a wide range of wild plants and animals?

17 What collective name is sometimes given to a flock of larks on the wing?

18 There was great excitement among biologists in 1938 when a strange, prehistoric-looking fish was caught in the Indian Ocean. What is this fish called?

19 What is the common name of the tree with the scientific name *Ginkgo biloba*?

20 What are keas (kay-as) and kakapos (kak-er-pose)?

1 The wolf

2 Iceland – of course!

3 37°C

4 The National Trust

5 The froghopper

6 Bright yellow

7 The pouch of a kangaroo or other marsupial mammal

8 The box: it is an evergreen tree and the others are deciduous

9 Twice every month – at the time of new and full moons

10 The wren

11 Kidney shaped

12 Bonsai

13 An ibex is a wild goat, but an ibis is a long-legged wading bird

14 Florets

15 Its nostril or breathing hole

16 Richard Mabey

17 An exaltation, although it is rarely used now

18 A coelacanth

19 The maidenhair tree (accept ginkgo)

20 New Zealand parrots: the kakapo is nocturnal and flightless and sometimes called the owl parrot

QUIZ 21

1 Cod–liver oil is actually obtained from coconuts: true or false?

2 Which prehistoric age has divisions known as the Palaeolithic (Pal-ee-oh-lithic), Mesolithic and Neolithic?

3 What does biodegradable mean?

4 Scree is the natural home of many beautiful rock plants. What is scree?

5 What is an animal's cranium?

6 In horse breeding, the male parent or stallion is called the sire, but what is the female parent called?

7 What do we call the gravelly bed in which a salmon lays its eggs?

8 What is the common name of the insect whose scientific name is *Apis mellifera*?

9 What collective name is sometimes given to a group of vipers?

10 Ludwig Koch was a well-known broadcaster in the 1940s and 1950s. What was his speciality?

11 From what kind of tree do we get turpentine?

12 What are chows, borzois and samoyeds?

13 What is a baobab?

14 How did the processionary moth gets its name?

15 Which is the odd one out: gharial, gecko, caiman, capercaillie?

16 Where did the potato originate?

17 How does the archer fish capture its prey?

18 Why do farmers not like spindle in their hedges?

19 What animals belong to the family Talpidae?

20 What common garden weed is known as cluckenweed in some northern areas?

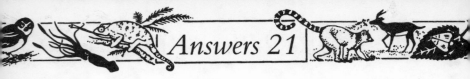
1 False: it really does come from the cod's liver

2 The Stone Age

3 A biodegradable material can be decomposed and destroyed by natural means – by the action of fungi and bacteria, for example

4 Loose rock fragments that accumulate at the foot of cliffs, especially in mountain areas

5 Its skull

6 The dam

7 A redd

8 The honey bee

9 A nest

10 He specialised in recording the sounds of birds and other animals

11 Pine trees

12 Breeds of dogs

13 A tree, famous for its barrel-like, water-storing trunk

14 Because the caterpillars travel nose-to-tail in single file when they go out to feed. The best known is the pine processionary, whose caterpillars live in large silken nests and cause serious damage to pine trees in southern Europe

15 The capercaillie: it is a bird and the others are all reptiles

16 South America

17 It fires a stream of water droplets at insects resting on plants overhanging the water. The jet knocks the insects into the water, where the fish can grab them

18 The spindle is one of the shrubs on which blackfly lay their winter eggs – and blackfly is a serious pest of beans and sugar beet

19 Moles

20 Chickweed

QUIZ 22

1 What sort of animal is a boomslang?

2 Name Britain's smallest butterfly

3 What animal is affectionately known as brock?

4 How do insect-eating bats find their prey?

5 What is symbiosis?

6 Blackberries, apples and strawberries all belong to the rose family: true or false?

7 How many legs does an okapi have?

8 What is a witches' broom?

9 What kind of wood was traditionally used to make rulers?

10 Where would you go to find an oysterplant?

11 What name is given to a group of ferrets?

12 What are oviparous animals?

13 To what family of moths do looper caterpillars belong?

14 What is a water soldier?

15 What do speleologists (spee-lee-ologists) study?

16 How many teats does a billy goat have?

17 The dachshund is a popular pet, but what does its name really mean?

18 What is the sole food of the koala?

19 What kind of fish has a prehensile tail?

20 On what do wasps feed their grubs?

1 A snake

2 The small blue, also called the little blue

3 The badger

4 By sending out high-pitched sounds and listening to the echoes bouncing back from the insects. This method is called echo-location

5 The word means living together, and is usually used to refer to a partnership between two different kinds of animals or plants in which both partners benefit from the association

6 True

7 Four: it is a mammal related to the giraffe

8 It is an abnormal growth or gall on a tree or shrub, consisting of a dense cluster of twigs. It is usually brought about when a fungus invades the tree

9 Box wood, because it is very hard and does not warp or shrink

10 The seashore

11 A business

12 Animals that lay eggs

13 The geometer family or Geometridae

14 A spiky water plant

15 Caves and cave life

16 None: a billy goat is a male!

17 Badger-hound

18 Eucalyptus leaves

19 The seahorse

20 Flesh of various kinds, especially that of other insects

QUIZ 23

1 Name the family in which father, mother and son have done so much to unearth man's ancestors in East Africa in recent decades

2 What kind of organism is a liverwort?

3 Amber is fossilised resin from coniferous trees: true or false?

4 Name the sugary substance secreted by flowers to attract insects

5 Which is the odd one out: slow-worm, earthworm, ragworm, leech?

6 Why is a pit-viper so called?

7 What is the main gas involved in global warming or the greenhouse effect?

8 What colour are the flowers of winter aconite?

9 Which has more teeth – a cat or a dog?

10 Apart from man, what is the only primate living wild in Europe?

11 Where is the original home of the cocoa or cacao tree?

12 What insects belong to the family Sphingidae (Sfing-giddy)?

13 What trees can be silver, noble, or grand?

14 What is a beck?

15 Where would you go to find wild swallowtail butterflies in Britain?

16 How many arms has a squid?

17 Name the world's largest rodent

18 What is the more familiar name of *Atropa belladonna*?

19 Why is the slipper limpet a serious pest of oyster beds?

20 Would you be pleased to entertain *Serpula lachrymans* in your house?

1 The Leakey family

2 A low-growing flowerless plant related to the mosses

3 True

4 Nectar

5 The slow-worm: it is a lizard and the others are true worms

6 Because it has heat-sensitive pits on its face that help it to track down its warm-blooded prey

7 Carbon dioxide

8 Yellow

9 A dog: the dog normally has 42 teeth, while the cat, with its much shorter muzzle, has only 30 teeth

10 The Barbary ape – a tailless monkey living on the Rock of Gibraltar

11 The tropical forests of South America

12 Hawkmoths

13 Fir trees

14 A small, fast-flowing stream

15 The Norfolk Broads or the East Anglian Fens

16 Ten: eight short ones and two long ones that can be shot out to capture prey

17 The capybara of South America

18 Deadly nightshade

19 Because it clings to the oyster shells and cuts off their food supplies by taking them itself

20 No: it is the dry-rot fungus!

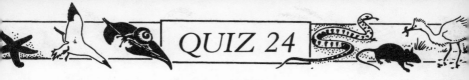

1 What is the national flower of Austria?

2 How did the comma butterfly gets its name?

3 What, in the botanical world, are wracks?

4 What do the letters IUCN stand for?

5 What are shoddy aliens?

6 What is the name given to the method by which grasshoppers and crickets make their calls?

7 Name the shiny bristletail that scuttles about in our houses at night

8 What is the principal food of a robber-fly?

9 What shape are sagittate leaves?

10 What collective name is given to a group of foxes?

11 What is a dimorphic species?

12 What was the name of the *Children's Hour* radio programme in which famous naturalists answered listeners' questions?

13 Cobs and filberts are varieties of which tree?

14 What is the main difference between monkeys and apes?

15 A kangaroo is about as big as a runner bean seed when it is born: true or false?

16 Where does the bitterling fish lay its eggs?

17 What is unusual about the beak of the skimmer?

18 What do larks, eagles and treecreepers all have in common?

19 Name the largest lake in the United Kingdom

20 What name do we give to a female fallow deer?

1 Edelweiss

2 From the white, comma-shaped mark under its hindwing

3 Brown seaweeds

4 International Union for Conservation of Nature and Natural Resources

5 Foreign plants that have arrived in this country as seeds in consignments of wool and have become established in the countryside — especially around the wool towns. Shoddy is a name for wool waste

6 Stridulation

7 The silverfish

8 Other insects, which the robber-fly usually catches in flight

9 Arrowhead-shaped

10 A skulk

11 A species that exists in two distinct forms

12 Nature Parliament

13 Hazel

14 Monkeys usually have tails: apes do not

15 True

16 Inside the shell of a living freshwater mussel

17 The lower half is longer than the upper half

18 All three groups of birds include species called short-toed

19 Lough Neagh in Northern Ireland

20 A doe

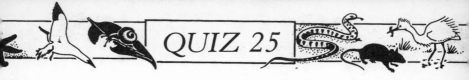

1 A deceit is the collective term applied to groups of which common bird?

2 What name is given to all the plant life of a region or country?

3 What name is given to the cud–chewing animals?

4 How did the bloody-nosed beetle get its name?

5 Where would you find a weever fish?

6 Why would most people rather not find weever fishes?

7 What tree has the scientific name *Ilex aquifolium*?

8 Which group of moths has varieties called scarlet, wood, Jersey and ruby?

9 What is a trilobite?

10 The male stag beetle's antlers are really huge jaws: true or false?

11 What is the proper name for a sea urchin's shell?

12 What is a female swan called?

13 Name two butterflies that regularly sleep through the winter in Britain as adults

14 What is the national flower of Scotland?

15 What is an elver?

16 Which famous zoological society was formed in 1826?

17 What sort of animal is a viscacha (viss-catcher)?

18 Is the white rhinoceros really white?

19 What sort of insect is a water boatman?

20 Name the strongly scented vegetation, dominated by large heaths and cistus bushes, that covers large areas of Corsica and other Mediterranean islands

1 The lapwing

2 Flora

3 Ruminants

4 Because it exudes a drop of bright red fluid from its mouth when alarmed

5 In shallow seas, usually on sandy bottoms close to the shore

6 Because the fishes have venomous spines on the back and can cause great pain if they are trodden on

7 The holly

8 Tiger moths

9 An extinct animal known only as fossils. There were a great many species, living in the sea and looking rather like woodlice

10 True

11 A test

12 A pen

13 Any two from brimstone, comma, peacock, small tortoiseshell and large tortoiseshell, although the last species may well be extinct in Britain

14 The thistle

15 A young eel

16 The Zoological Society of London – the society that owns London Zoo

17 A South American rodent

18 No: it is grey, just like the black rhinoceros! The name white is a corruption of an Afrikaans word meaning wide, and refers to the animal's broad snout

19 An aquatic bug

20 The maquis

1 Who designed the huge aviary opened at London Zoo in 1965?

2 What birds have species called eagle, scops and snowy?

3 What sort of plant is wall rue?

4 What do the initials SSSI mean in the context of nature conservation?

5 What kind of animal is a remora?

6 How many petals does a wild rose normally have?

7 What is the world's largest land-living carnivore?

8 What kinds of insects make up the family Formicidae?

9 What name do we give to a female hedgehog?

10 What happens to goldfish if they are kept in the dark for a long period?

11 Greyhounds were originally bred for hunting what kind of animal?

12 After whom is the Fuchsia named?

13 What is a ruderal plant?

14 Where do littoral animals live?

15 What, on a fish, can be anal, pectoral, or pelvic?

16 Are mute swans really mute?

17 Which tree is associated with the Sunday before Easter?

18 Jacques Cousteau regularly appeared on TV with his boat the Calypso. What was his profession?

19 Hoddy-doddy is a country name for which common garden animal?

20 What collective name is sometimes applied to a group of moles?

1 Lord Snowdon

2 Owls

3 A small fern, usually growing on rocks and walls

4 Site of Special Scientific Interest

5 A fish that hitches lifts on larger fishes by clinging to them with a powerful sucker on the top of its head

6 Five

7 The Kodiak bear – one of the races of the brown bear, living on the Kodiak Islands in Alaska. Males have been known to weigh as much as one tonne (2200 lb) and to stand 3.4 m (11 ft 1 in) high on their back legs

8 Ants

9 A sow

10 They turn white

11 Hares

12 Leonhard Fuchs, a 16th-century German botanist

13 Any plant characteristic of waste ground or any other area, such as a roadside, disturbed by human activity

14 On the seashore or on the shores of lakes

15 Fins

16 No: they can make various hissing and grunting sounds but, unlike most other swans, they are silent in flight

17 The palm tree: the Sunday is called Palm Sunday

18 A marine biologist

19 A snail

20 A labour

1 Where must you go in Britain to see genuine wildcats?

2 What is the more familiar name of *Solanum tuberosum*?

3 During which period of the earth's history were most of our coal fields formed?

4 The speckled wood butterfly rarely visits flowers, so what does it use for food?

5 What is a pudu?

6 Eels can reach new streams by wriggling over land at night: true or false?

7 Name the world's largest bird of prey

8 What is the major food of the green woodpecker?

9 What are listed in the Red Data Books?

10 What are the principal kinds of plants in the family Ericaceae?

11 What is parthenogenesis?

12 From which animal's milk was mozzarella cheese originally made?

13 Where do Arctic terns go for the northern winter?

14 Why were canaries kept in coal mines?

15 What do conchologists (con–col–ogists) study?

16 What colour are the flowers of the bladder campion?

17 How many humps does a new-born camel have?

18 What collective name is sometimes given to a group of nightingales?

19 Which group of birds includes species called reed, corn and snow?

20 The ugli is a citrus fruit originating as a hybrid between a tangerine and which other fruit?

1 To Scotland

2 The potato

3 The Carboniferous Period, roughly 300 million years ago

4 The honeydew dropped by aphids and other sap-feeding bugs

5 A small South American deer

6 True

7 The Andean condor: it weighs up to 14 kg (31 lb) and its wings span up to 3.2 m (10 ft 6 in.)

8 Ants

9 Endangered species

10 Heaths or heathers

11 Virgin birth – the ability of female animals to give birth or to lay fertile eggs without mating. It occurs mainly in insects

12 Water buffalo milk

13 The Antarctic

14 To give warning of a build-up of harmful gases

15 Shells

16 White

17 None

18 A watch

19 Buntings

20 The grapefruit

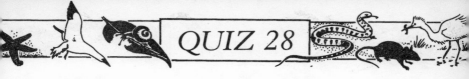

QUIZ 28

1 What colour are the young twigs of the dogwood?

2 Pineapples grow on trees that originally came from South America: true or false?

3 What is a xerophyte?

4 What sort of animal is a silkworm?

5 How many legs does a centipede have on each segment of its body?

6 What is the better known name of the cachalot?

7 What is the difference between poisonous and venomous animals?

8 What do scatologists open up?

9 What animals can be horseshoe, long-eared, or free-tailed?

10 Where is the Coto Doñana National Park, famous for its incredibly rich bird life?

11 From what kind of tree do we get cork?

12 What sort of food do piscivorous (pis-iv-er-us) animals eat?

13 What is the proper name for the parachute of hairs on top of the seeds of dandelions and related plants?

14 How many arms or tentacles has an octopus?

15 What is a sea gooseberry?

16 In America this plant is called alfalfa: what do we usually call it in Britain?

17 Which is the odd one out: heath violet, marsh violet, water violet, fen violet?

18 What is the alternative common name of the hedge brown butterfly?

19 To which family does the mynah bird belong?

20 What is an oast house?

1 Purplish-red (accept red or purple)

2 False: pineapples grow close to the ground on short herbaceous plants, although they did originally come from South America

3 A plant adapted for life in dry places, such as deserts

4 It is the caterpillar of a moth

5 Two

6 The sperm whale

7 Venomous animals have weapons with which to fire or inject venom or poison: poisonous animals merely have poison in their bodies and are harmful only when eaten

8 Animal droppings. Scat is another word for a dropping

9 Bats

10 Spain

11 The cork oak

12 Fish

13 A pappus

14 Eight

15 A small marine animal with a globular jelly-like body rather like a marble. It drifts at the surface of the sea and is often washed up on the beach

16 Lucerne

17 The water violet: it belongs to the primrose family and is not a violet at all

18 Gatekeeper

19 The starling family

20 A building used for drying hops

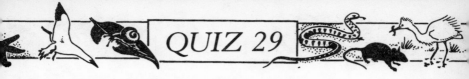

QUIZ 29

1 What do the Americans usually call stick insects?

2 How many legs does the small tortoiseshell butterfly use for walking?

3 Name a kind of animal that travels about in pod

4 What is a biennial plant?

5 The green woodpecker's tongue is half as long as its body: true or false?

6 What is the timber line or tree line?

7 What flowers have varieties called musk, melancholy, meadow and marsh?

8 Elephants, hippos and rhinos are sometimes called pachyderms. What does pachyderm mean?

9 How does the Australian mallee fowl incubate its eggs?

10 What common and harmless insect is often known as a horse-stinger or devil's darning needle?

11 What domestic animals have breeds known as Swaledales, Suffolks and Clun Forests?

12 Penicillin is obtained from a green mould, but who first discovered its anti-bacterial activity?

13 What was *Triceratops*?

14 What is a compound leaf?

15 What kind of creature is an axolotl?

16 What tree is the national emblem of Canada?

17 What is the main component of an ant's sting that causes the pain?

18 What do we call a male honey bee?

19 Does the common bindweed twine clockwise or anticlockwise as it climbs its support?

20 Which wild bird is the ancestor of all our town pigeons?

1 Walking sticks

2 Four: the front legs of this butterfly and other members of its family are very small and brush-like, and the insects are often called 'brush-footed butterflies'

3 Whales, dolphins and porpoises (accept seals also)

4 A plant that takes two growing seasons to complete its life cycle: it grows from seed and stores up food in the first year and then flowers and dies in the second. Carrots and parsnips are familiar examples

5 True

6 The line on a mountain or in the Arctic beyond which it is too cold for trees to grow

7 Thistles

8 Thick-skinned

9 It lays its eggs in a mound of decaying leaves and sand and the heat produced by the rotting leaves is enough to incubate the eggs

10 The dragonfly

11 Sheep

12 Sir Alexander Fleming

13 A dinosaur with three horns

14 A leaf that is split up into several leaflets all coming from the same stalk. Ash and horse chestnut leaves are common examples

15 It is a Mexican salamander, but it is a very unusual animal because it never really grows up: it stays in the tadpole stage all its life, although its sex organs develop and it can reproduce

16 The Maple

17 Formic acid

18 A drone

19 Anticlockwise

20 The rock dove

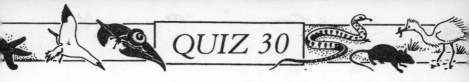

QUIZ 30

1 What kind of animal was Tarka in Henry Williamson's famous story?

2 What large butterfly, occasionally seen in Britain, is also known as the milkweed?

3 What country at the eastern end of the Mediterranean has a cedar named after it?

4 What animal is scientifically known as *Canis familiaris*?

5 What happens in a bird's gizzard?

6 What do we call dried plums?

7 What might a tree-lover do with a cobbler's heel ball and a sheet of paper?

8 What are hammerheads and threshers?

9 What is a liger?

10 How many toes normally point forward on a robin's foot?

11 How has the beetle *Scolytus scolytus* changed the face of the British countryside in recent decades?

12 Name the area of clays and sandstones between the North and South Downs

13 What do leafcutter ants eat?

14 What is the basic shape of a snowflake?

15 What is the name of the process by which plant leaves give off water vapour?

16 Which bird is said to boom?

17 Brazil nuts originally came from Indochina: true or false?

18 What is the gestation period of a mouse?

19 What is silviculture?

20 What name is given to a group of rooks?

1 An otter

2 The monarch

3 Lebanon

4 The domestic dog

5 Grain and other tough food is crushed and ground up with the aid of grit or small stones swallowed by the bird

6 Prunes

7 Make bark rubbings

8 Sharks

9 A cross or hybrid between a male lion and a female tiger. A cross between a male tiger and a female lion is called a tigon

10 Three

11 By carrying Dutch elm disease, the fungus disease that has killed millions of elm trees

12 The Weald

13 Fungi or moulds, that the ants cultivate on beds of chewed leaves

14 Hexagonal or six-sided

15 Transpiration

16 The bittern – because of its deep, booming call

17 False: they originated in Brazil

18 About 3 weeks

19 The cultivation of trees (accept forestry)

20 A building or a parliament

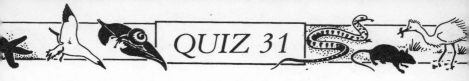

1 Where in England can you see the Whin Sill?

2 What animal is depicted in the famous painting *The Monarch of the Glen*?

3 Name the scale used to measure and record wind velocities

4 What do the caterpillars of most hawkmoths have at the rear ends of their bodies?

5 Where would you find pronghorns in the wild?

6 What colour are the buds of the ash tree?

7 What birds can be glaucous, ivory, or black-headed?

8 Which wild flower, producing an edible fruit, has the scientific name *Fragaria vesca*?

9 To what family of plants does the sugar cane belong?

10 What animal is the mother of a mule?

11 What are Blenheim Orange, Worcester Pearmain and Laxton's Superb?

12 Newts lay their eggs in long chains: true or false?

13 Where does the rattlesnake carry its rattle?

14 What do we call the early stages in the growth of seeds and seedlings?

15 Marjorie Blamey is a well-known artist specialising in what?

16 What is the common name of the insect whose scientific name is *Pieris brassicae*?

17 What do we call the process by which rocks are gradually broken down by the elements and the action of plant roots?

18 How many toes does an ostrich have?

19 What do coprophagous (cop-roe-fay-gus) animals eat?

20 What name is given to a young pigeon?

1 In the north of England. It is a layer of very hard volcanic rock forming a wall-like line of crags and cliffs across the country from the Northumberland coast to Cumbria. Many parts of Hadrian's Wall stand on it

2 A red deer (accept stag)

3 The Beaufort Scale

4 A curved horn

5 The Prairies of North America

6 Black

7 Gulls

8 The wild strawberry

9 The grass family (accept Poaceae or Gramineae – the old name for the family)

10 A horse: a mule is the offspring of a male donkey and a female horse

11 Varieties of eating apples

12 False: newts lay their eggs singly, wrapping each one in a folded leaf

13 At the end of its tail

14 Germination

15 Wild flowers

16 The large white butterfly (accept cabbage white)

17 Weathering

18 Four – two on each foot

19 Dung

20 A squab

1 What are Grimes Graves?

2 What popular strong drink is flavoured with juniper?

3 What do the letters NNR mean?

4 What animal has species known as Burchell's, Grevy's and mountain?

5 What colour are most gentian flowers?

6 How does the female orange-tip butterfly differ in appearance from the male?

7 Name the world's smallest bird

8 What is the alternative, older name for our lime trees?

9 What kind of animal is a piddock?

10 How does the chameleon catch its prey?

11 What is a destroying angel?

12 Oak apples and robins' pincushions are examples of what kinds of growth?

13 What is the main food of the short-toed eagle?

14 Where would you find the world's only truly marine lizards?

15 To which family does the llama belong?

16 How did the horseshoe vetch gets its name?

17 Which birds come together in convocations?

18 Warble-flies attack what kinds of animals?

19 What is a thorn-apple?

20 The male seahorse gives birth to the babies: true or false?

1 Stone-age flint mines near Thetford in Norfolk

2 Gin

3 National Nature Reserve

4 Zebras

5 Blue

6 She does not have orange tips to her wings

7 The bee hummingbird of Cuba: it is under 6 cm (2.4 in) long and weighs about 1.6 grammes (0.06 oz)

8 Linden trees

9 A bivalve mollusc that tunnels into rocks (accept seashell)

10 It fires out its long, sticky tongue to grab insects and other small prey

11 A very poisonous toadstool or fungus

12 Plant galls

13 Snakes

14 On the Galapagos Islands in the Pacific Ocean: they are the marine iguanas and they feed on seaweeds

15 The camel family (accept Camelidae)

16 Because the seed pods break up into tiny horseshoe-shaped sections

17 Eagles

18 Cattle and deer

19 A poisonous plant, related to the potato and named for its spiky fruits

20 True: the female lays her eggs in a pouch on the male's belly and he gives birth to the babies when the eggs have hatched

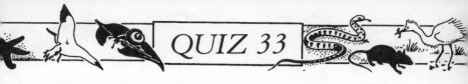

1 What are Belted Galloways, Lincoln Reds and Welsh Blacks?

2 In what field did Mary Anning of Lyme Regis make a name for herself in the 19th century?

3 Which insect transmits sleeping sickness?

4 What is a smolt?

5 The ostrich, rhea and emu are not closely related, but they look very much alike. Why?

6 What do we call the offspring of two different parental species?

7 Where do most of the world's marsupials live?

8 What is a pinnate leaf?

9 A sponge is a simple kind of plant: true or false?

10 To what class of animals do barnacles belong?

11 How many species of fish are there in the world: approximately 1000, 12,000, 20,000, or 40,000?

12 What is the colouring of the cinnabar moth?

13 What kind of habitat would you visit to gather cloudberries?

14 What kind of animal is a sand dollar?

15 Where is the Kruger National Park?

16 What is wrong with the following diary entry? 'I chipped away at a large boulder of granite and it eventually split open to reveal the perfectly preserved fossil of a fish.'

17 What colour is the leopard moth?

18 What animal was once used by doctors to remove blood from sick patients in the belief that the blood-letting would cure various illnesses?

19 What exactly are reindeer moss, pixie cups and sea ivory?

20 Which is the odd one out: restharrow, ragged robin, evening primrose, rosebay willowherb?

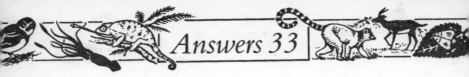

1 Breeds of cattle

2 She was very good at finding fossils and was the first person to discover a more or less complete ichthyosaur fossil – when she was only eleven

3 The tsetse-fly

4 A young salmon

5 Because they have all become adapted, independently, for a life of running on the grasslands – the ostrich in Africa, the rhea in South America and the emu in Australia

6 A hybrid

7 In Australia

8 A compound leaf whose leaflets arise in pairs on opposite sides of the central stalk. The ash leaf is a good example

9 False: a sponge is an animal

10 The Crustacea or crustaceans – the same group as the crabs and shrimps

11 Approximately 20,000

12 Black and red

13 Bogs or moorland: the cloudberry looks like a golden or orange blackberry and grows close to the ground, mainly in the north

14 A very flat sea urchin

15 South Africa

16 Granite formed from molten rock deep in the earth's crust and therefore cannot contain fossils

17 Black and white

18 The leech

19 Lichens

20 The evening primrose – on two counts: it has yellow flowers and it is not native in Europe (it came from North America). The other plants are all natives and have pink flowers

QUIZ 34

1 What do we call the vast expanse of windswept, treeless land fringing the Arctic Ocean?

2 A plant growing where it is not wanted is a common definition of what?

3 On a bird, what can be primary, secondary, or covert?

4 Which is the odd–one–out: otter, zebra, lion, horse?

5 What do we call a stoat in its winter coat?

6 What is a calcifuge (cal-see-fewj) plant?

7 The mammoth was an extinct relative of which living mammal?

8 What is the smallest British member of the carp family?

9 What colour is the crown of a green woodpecker?

10 How does a hamster carry food back to its nest?

11 What important fibre do we get from the leaves of agave plants?

12 Where are you most likely to find caterpillars of the death's-head hawkmoth in Britain?

13 Name two British birds whose names contain the names of seashore animals

14 What are fairies' bonnets?

15 Who wrote the award-winning book *The History of the Countryside*?

16 From what region of an insect's body do the wings grow?

17 What is the primary function of the prickles of roses and brambles?

18 The names of all animal families end in what four letters?

19 What colour are the fruits of the spindle tree?

20 What name is given to a colony of penguins?

1 The tundra

2 A weed

3 Feathers

4 Zebra: the others can follow 'sea' to give the names of three new animals

5 Ermine

6 A plant that cannot tolerate lime

7 The elephant

8 The minnow

9 Red

10 In fur-lined pouches inside its mouth

11 Sisal, which is used to make ropes and string

12 In potato fields because the caterpillars feed mainly on potato leaves

13 Barnacle goose and oyster catcher

14 Toadstools or fungi

15 Oliver Rackham

16 The thorax

17 Climbing: the prickles are generally curved and they hold the plants up by hooking over neighbouring twigs

18 -idae

19 Pink, with bright orange seeds inside them

20 A rookery

QUIZ 35

1 A pair of binoculars is marked 8 x 40: what does the figure 40 mean?

2 What Australian trees can be red river, ribbon, or snow?

3 What are Long Meg and her Daughters?

4 Butterflies chew pollen when they visit flowers: true or false?

5 What is a squirting cucumber?

6 What, in the field of natural history, is General Sherman?

7 Where do European eels go to spawn?

8 How do termite colonies differ in their make-up from those of ants?

9 What birds may go about in small groups called tidings?

10 What is an annual plant?

11 How did the painter's mussel get its name?

12 Name the longest river in British Isles

13 What is the proper name for an insect's feelers?

14 What bee cuts pieces from the leaves of roses and other plants?

15 What is the main food of the glow-worm?

16 What use do the leaves of sweet cicely have in the kitchen?

17 What do the following all have in common apart from being flowers: anemone, crane's-bill and spurge?

18 What is carpology, also known as pomology?

19 How many humps does a Bactrian camel have?

20 What is a male goose called?

1 It means that the diameter of the objective lens is 40 mm, the objective being the lens furthest from your eyes

2 Gum trees or eucalyptus trees

3 A circle of prehistoric standing stones in the Vale of Eden in Cumbria

4 False: butterflies have no jaws and can only suck up liquids

5 A plant named for the way its egg-shaped fruit squirts out its seeds in a jet of slime when they are ripe

6 It is a huge specimen of the giant sequoia tree and probably the largest living thing on earth

7 The Sargasso Sea in the western Atlantic Ocean

8 Termite colonies contain more or less equal numbers of males and females: ant colonies consist almost entirely of females

9 Magpies

10 A plant that grows from seed, flowers, and dies within the space of one year — and often very much less. Some desert plants complete their lives in just a few weeks

11 Because artists used its shells to hold and mix their paints

12 The Shannon in Ireland

13 Antennae

14 The leafcutter bee

15 Snails: adult glow-worms do not feed much, but their larvae feed on snails

16 They can be used to sweeten rhubarb, gooseberries and other acidic foods by taking the sharpness away

17 They all have species called wood — wood anemone, etc

18 The study of fruits

19 Two

20 A gander

QUIZ 36

1 What is the world's fastest bird?

2 Where would you find mangrove swamps?

3 What is a dryad's saddle?

4 What colour are the flowers of biting stonecrop?

5 What animals can be smooth, warty, or marbled?

6 What do we call a beaver's home?

7 Does the Arctic fox have larger or smaller ears than the red fox?

8 What frightened Miss Muffet?

9 What are the three main colours of seaweeds?

10 Americans call it the fall: what do we call it in Britain?

11 Name a British bird that has the name of a fish in its name

12 What shape is a palmate leaf?

13 Name the ship on which Charles Darwin made his round-the-world voyage

14 What is the function of a fish's gills?

15 What sort of animal is a hartebeeste?

16 From which country did the Lhasa Apso dog originate?

17 What are otter spraints?

18 What small plants have been used to monitor and map air pollution?

19 Where can porcupines be found living wild in Europe?

20 What kinds of birds are sometimes described as raptors?

1 The peregrine falcon: when swooping down to catch prey it can reach 180 kmph (112 mph)

2 Around tropical coasts and estuaries

3 A large bracket fungus growing on tree trunks

4 Yellow

5 Newts

6 A lodge

7 Smaller. Arctic mammals generally have smaller ears than their relatives in warmer countries, because less heat is lost through small ears. They tend to have shorter legs and muzzles for the same reason

8 A spider

9 Green, brown and red

10 Autumn

11 Herring gull

12 Hand-shaped, with the main veins fanning out like the palm and fingers of your hand. The sycamore leaf is a good example

13 The Beagle

14 They are its breathing organs, absorbing oxygen from the water and passing it to the blood-stream

15 An African antelope

16 Tibet

17 The animal's droppings

18 Lichens, most of which are unable to tolerate air pollution

19 Italy

20 Birds of prey

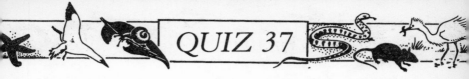

1 What group of insects includes species called carpet, furniture and larder?

2 For what bird is Abbotsbury in Dorset famous?

3 What name is given to hot springs that periodically shoot water high into the air?

4 There are only about 25 living members of the genus *Equisetum* in the world: what is their common name?

5 What does a female cricket do with her ovipositor?

6 What colour are the ripe fruits of bittersweet?

7 What is a miller's thumb?

8 What do we call young frogs and toads?

9 What is the more familiar name for furze?

10 Which British crow is largely brown with a blue flash on each side?

11 What colour are the flowers of the bird's-eye primrose?

12 What is the literal meaning of the name daisy?

13 How much water can a camel hold in its hump?

14 What is a brown turkey?

15 What is a turkey brown?

16 After whom was the dahlia named?

17 What are viviparous animals?

18 What colour is a moorhen's beak?

19 *Vitis vinifera* is cultivated in many countries and is the basis of a multi-million-pound industry: what is its common name?

20 Ivy is a death-dealing parasite: true or false?

1 Beetles

2 The mute swan: Benedictine monks established a swannery at Abbotsbury over 600 years ago and swans have been reared there ever since. The swannery is open to the public in the summer

3 Geysers

4 Horsetails

5 She lays her eggs with it

6 Red

7 A freshwater fish, also known as a bullhead

8 Tadpoles

9 Gorse

10 The jay

11 Pink

12 The day's eye, referring to the fact that the flowers open when the sun rises and close when it sets

13 None: the hump is a store of fat

14 A cultivated variety of fig

15 An angler's name for a small mayfly

16 A Swedish botanist called Anders Dahl

17 Animals that give birth to live young, as opposed to laying eggs

18 Red and yellow: it is mainly red, with a yellow tip

19 The grape-vine

20 False: although the ivy may compete with other plants for water and air, it does not steal anything directly from the trees on which it climbs and is not a parasite. It can live happily on walls without any other plants

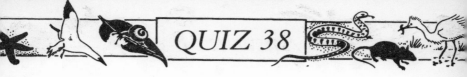

1 What is a smew?

2 Name the large marshy area at the mouth of the River Rhône in France, famous for its flamingos and wild horses

3 Glutton is the alternative name for which carnivorous mammal?

4 What can be beefsteak, oyster, or orange-peel?

5 What do the letters YOC stand for?

6 What is a flyway?

7 Percy Edwards was a well-known broadcaster: what was his particular expertise?

8 What are lammas leaves?

9 Where does the great grey slug mate?

10 What colour are linseed flowers?

11 In botanical terms, what is the essential difference between a sweet chestnut and a horse chestnut or conker?

12 What insects belong to the genus Bombus?

13 What is the commoner or more familiar name for a sea swallow?

14 What name is usually given to a young seal?

15 What kinds of animals make up the avifauna of a region?

16 What is pisciculture?

17 How many eyes does an earthworm have?

18 What gives carrots their characteristic orange or red colour?

19 How did the potter wasp get its name?

20 What kind of plant is a twayblade?

1 A kind of duck

2 The Camargue

3 The wolverine

4 Fungi

5 Young Ornithologists' Club

6 A regular route used by migrating birds

7 He did animal impersonations, including superb renderings of bird songs

8 A second crop of leaves produced late in the season, especially by oak trees that have been attacked by caterpillars and have lost many of their original leaves

9 In the air, suspended on a thick rope of slime attached to a tree or other support

10 Blue

11 The sweet chestnut is a fruit, but the conker is a seed

12 Bumble bees

13 Tern

14 A pup

15 Birds

16 Fish-rearing

17 None

18 Carotene

19 Because it builds little clay pots or vases as nests for its offspring

20 An orchid

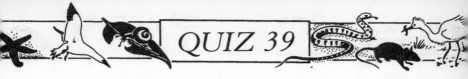

QUIZ 39

1 What is the most obvious difference between a heron and a stork in flight?

2 Which of the day's meals would you most likely be eating if you were tucking into a dish of *Avena sativa* and a plate of smoked *Clupea harengus*?

3 What is a capon?

4 Where is Cape Wrath?

5 What do the following have in common: stock, pea, bindweed, holly?

6 What is cynophobia?

7 In botanical terms, what is a Brussels sprout?

8 What animal's name means 'horse of the river'?

9 What is unusual about the roots of peas and beans and other members of the family Fabaceae?

10 What is a gharial?

11 Can earwigs fly?

12 What is an epiphyte?

13 To what group of invertebrate animals do the ticks belong?

14 What are large whites, large blacks and saddlebacks?

15 Name the parson who wrote *The Natural History of Selborne*

16 What are contour lines on maps?

17 What do we call the delicate radiating flaps under the cap of a mushroom?

18 In what sport might you see an eagle or an albatross?

19 From what plant do we obtain linen?

20 What colour is the head of a male pochard?

1 The heron bends its neck and pulls its head back to its shoulders, but the stork flies with its neck straight

2 Breakfast: *Avena sativa* is oats (porridge) and smoked *Clupea harengus* is a kipper

3 A castrated cockerel

4 It is the extreme tip of north-west Scotland

5 All can be preceded by sea to give the names of more plants

6 Fear of dogs

7 A large bud

8 The hippopotamus

9 They are covered with nodules containing bacteria that help the plants to augment their supplies of nitrogen

10 A reptile closely related to the crocodile family

11 Yes, although not all species have wings

12 A plant that grows perched on another without taking any food from it. Lichens and ferns growing on trees are good examples

13 The arachnids, which are a class of the arthropods

14 Breeds of pig

15 Gilbert White

16 Lines joining places of equal height above sea level

17 Gills

18 Golf

19 Flax

20 Chestnut brown

QUIZ 40

1 Name the famous beechwood on the borders of Buckinghamshire and Berkshire, just to the west of London

2 To what theory did the French naturalist Jean Baptiste Lamarck make a major contribution, although his ideas were later disproved?

3 For what does a fisherman use a creel?

4 What is the difference between a tamarind and a tamarin?

5 Where, in the British Isles, can you find reindeer living in the wild?

6 Approximately how long has life been in existence on Earth: 10 million years, 10,000 million years, or 3,500 million years?

7 What are ungulate animals?

8 In which part of the world did the monkey puzzle tree originate?

9 How do frigate birds get most of their food?

10 What do the following birds have in common: cuckoo, nightingale, swallow?

11 What is the Mistral?

12 What kind of animal is the ringhals?

13 What is the world's heaviest insect?

14 Which birds, belonging to the crow family, live in groups called chatterings?

15 What is the more common name of the brandy bottle flower?

16 What does a shrike do with prey that is not eaten right away?

17 Some slugs have shells: true or false?

18 What is unusual about the group of mammals called monotremes?

19 What colour are ripe privet berries?

20 Oak trees have catkins: true or false?

1 Burnham Beeches

2 The theory of evolution

3 It is a net or basket for holding fish that have been caught

4 A tamarind is an edible fruit, often used for making drinks, but a tamarin is a small South American monkey

5 The Cairngorms in Scotland

6 3,500 million years

7 Hoofed mammals

8 South America: it is often called the Chile pine

9 They chase other seabirds and make them drop the fish they have caught

10 The are all summer visitors to Europe

11 A strong wind that blows down the Rhône Valley in France, especially in autumn and winter

12 It is a snake, also called the spitting cobra because it spits venom

13 The Goliath beetle of tropical Africa: it is a fist-sized insect weighing nearly 100 grams (3.5 oz)

14 Choughs

15 The yellow water lily, from the shape of its fruits

16 It impales it on a stout thorn, or even a barbed wire fence, just as a butcher hangs meat on a hook. Shrikes are sometimes called butcher birds because of this habit

17 True, although the shells are usually very small and perched right on the rear end

18 They lay eggs

19 Black

20 True, but they are less obvious than many other catkins because they open at the same time as the leaves

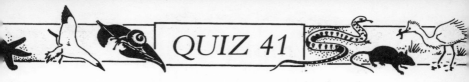

QUIZ 41

1 What name is normally given to a young deer?

2 What is the common name of the insect whose scientific name is *Mantis religiosa*?

3 Horses are measured in hands: how many inches are there in a hand?

4 What organisation produces the official maps of Britain?

5 What common plant's name literally means 'tooth of the lion'?

6 What is biological control?

7 What shape are an insect's antennae if they are technically described as claviform?

8 What animal lives in a drey?

9 How does a gardener normally refer to raspberry plants?

10 What sort of insects are locusts?

11 Thousands of whooper swans visit the British Isles for the winter and, as far as we know, they all come from the same country: which country?

12 What colour is a fire salamander?

13 What tree has been called 'nature's supermarket' because it provides so many useful products?

14 Name two European birds whose names each contain the name of a reptile

15 Vulpine is an adjective applied to which kinds of animals?

16 What group of butterflies have species called adonis, holly and silver-studded?

17 What famous landmark marks the eastern end of the South Downs?

18 What birds can be grey, purple, or night?

19 What familiar woodland and garden flower has the scientific name *Digitalis purpurea*?

20 What is aestivation?

1 A fawn

2 The praying mantis – so called because it holds its front legs up in front of its face, as if praying, while waiting for prey to arrive

3 Four

4 The Ordnance Survey

5 The dandelion, a corruption of the French 'dent de lion'

6 The use of natural enemies to control pests, a good example being the use of ladybirds to destroy aphids

7 Club-shaped

8 A squirrel

9 The gardener calls them canes

10 Large grasshoppers

11 Iceland

12 Black and yellow

13 The coconut palm

14 Turtle dove and snake eagle, although the latter is better known as the short-toed eagle

15 Foxes

16 The blues

17 Beachy Head

18 Herons

19 The foxglove

20 A summer sleep or dormant state, similar to hibernation, in which some animals, such as lungfishes, survive very hot or dry seasons

QUIZ 42

1 Name the only marsupial native to North America

2 Which is the odd one out: sea urchin, sea hare, cushion star, sea cucumber, feather star?

3 What would be the profession or interest of a person with the initials FRES after his or her name?

4 Where is the Negev Desert?

5 What do we call a cow who has not yet had a calf?

6 What do the following have in common: carrot, crane and house?

7 What kind of animal is an addax?

8 What is the more common name of the bedeguar gall?

9 Which insects belong to the order Odonata?

10 What tree with leaves rather like the sycamore is commonly planted in town streets and squares?

11 According to a popular song, what bird sang in London's Berkeley Square?

12 By what are the flowers of most grasses pollinated?

13 What is the largest true wasp in Britain?

14 What flowering plants have species called ivy-leaved, germander and wall?

15 What is the lightest of all timbers?

16 What is kelp?

17 Yeasts belong to which major group of organisms?

18 Only queen ants have wings: true or false?

19 What are the main foods of the oystercatcher?

20 In the world of flowers, what is a naked lady?

1 The Virginia opossum

2 The sea hare: it is a mollusc and the others are all echinoderms

3 Entomology or the study of insects: FRES stands for Fellow of the Royal Entomological Society of London

4 Israel

5 A heifer

6 They can all be followed by fly

7 An antelope from the Sahara desert

8 The robin's pincushion: it is the fluffy-looking gall found on wild roses

9 Dragonflies and damselflies

10 The plane tree

11 A nightingale

12 The wind

13 The hornet

14 Speedwells

15 Balsa wood

16 Seaweed – especially the larger kinds

17 Fungi

18 False: the males also have wings. The queens do not keep their wings for long: they break them off after their mating flights and are then wingless for the rest of their lives

19 Cockles and mussels: they rarely eat oysters, which normally live below low-tide level

20 A colchicum or meadow saffron. The flowers are known as naked ladies because they appear in the autumn after the leaves have died down

QUIZ 43

1 What are Buff Orpingtons and Plymouth Rocks?

2 What is the proper name of the daddy-long-legs?

3 Lake Myvatn is one of Europe's best bird-watching sites: in which country is it?

4 What are igneous rocks?

5 What insects belong to the order Neuroptera?

6 Why is the lapwing known as the butcher bird in some country areas?

7 What tree is sometimes called the trembling poplar?

8 Which came first in evolution – birds or mammals?

9 High Force, in Teesdale, is a famous what?

10 What organisation has its headquarters at The Lodge, at Sandy in Bedfordshire?

11 Excluding rare visitors, how many butterfly species regularly breed in the wild in the British Isles?

12 What sort of animal is a thorny devil?

13 What do the following plants all have in common: heliotrope, aconite and jasmine?

14 What does an ophiologist study?

15 Which major North American airport got its name from the large populations of geese in the region?

16 The Queen of ... Fritillary is a rare visitor to the British Isles. What is the missing word?

17 What is the alternative name of the mountain ash?

18 What is the normal colour of a harebell?

19 What is the main food of finches?

20 What are Braunton Burrows, Hickling Broad and Inverpolly?

1 Breeds of chickens

2 The crane-fly

3 Iceland

4 Rocks that have solidified from a molten state, either deep in the earth or on the surface after being pumped out by volcanic eruptions

5 Any of the following: lacewings, alder flies, snakeflies and antlions

6 Because its pure white belly and 'shoulder straps' are thought to resemble an old-fashioned butcher's apron

7 The aspen

8 Mammals – they first appeared about 210 million years ago, but birds did not appear until about 150 million years ago

9 Waterfall

10 The Royal Society for the Protection of Birds, or RSPB

11 58 (accept anything from 56 to 60 inclusive)

12 A very spiny lizard living in the Australian deserts

13 They can all be preceded by winter to form the names of other plants

14 Snakes

15 Gander in Newfoundland

16 Spain

17 The rowan

18 Blue

19 Seeds

20 National Nature Reserves – in Devon, Norfolk and the Scottish Highlands respectively

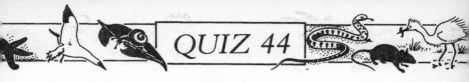

1 What is the national tree of Australia?

2 Which bird has the greatest wingspan?

3 What group of animals contains ghosts, hermits and robbers?

4 What is measured on the Richter Scale?

5 What name is given to the extensive grassy plains of temperate Asia and eastern Europe?

6 Which is the odd one out: elephant seal, Weddell seal, Solomon's seal, Ross seal?

7 Do coniferous trees yield hardwood or softwood?

8 What sort of bird is a muscovy?

9 As what colour are woodlands shown on Ordnance Survey maps?

10 On the coast of which county is Lulworth Cove?

11 What was the name of the famous elephant – probably the largest ever seen in captivity – who lived at London Zoo from 1865 until 1882 and then went to America to star in the Barnum & Bailey Circus?

12 In terms of the weather, what is the opposite of a depression?

13 What would you be about to eat if you ordered escargots in a restaurant?

14 What have fish, mushrooms and mussels in common?

15 What breed of dog is often called a spotted dick?

16 What bird has been called the crocodile's toothbrush?

17 What colour are the flowers of the flowering rush?

18 Name the only British bird with a white bill

19 Geoff Hamilton and Peter Seabrook are associated with what kind of TV programmes?

20 What is the alternative name of the thylacine, a large Australian carnivore that is now probably extinct?

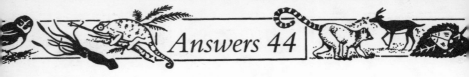

1 The golden wattle – a kind of mimosa or acacia

2 The wandering albatross, with a span of about 3.6 m (12 ft)

3 Crabs

4 The force or intensity of earthquakes

5 The Steppes

6 Solomon's seal: it is a plant

7 Softwood

8 A duck

9 Green

10 Dorset

11 Jumbo

12 An anticyclone

13 Snails

14 They all have gills

15 The Dalmatian

16 The Egyptian plover, which enters crocodiles' mouths and removes leeches and scraps of food from their teeth and gums (accept plover, as several other plovers have been reported to behave in this way.)

17 Pink

18 The coot

19 Gardening programmes

20 The Tasmanian wolf

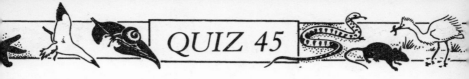

QUIZ 45

1. What is the Severn Bore?

2. What kind of bird is a lammergeier?

3. Toucans are natives of which continent?

4. To what family of plants do the cotton grasses belong?

5. What is a gribble?

6. Which is the largest of the British falcons?

7. Some mammals lay eggs: true or false?

8. What is the main food of the puffin?

9. What is a perennial plant?

10. Coffin-cutter, sow-bug, sink louse and tiggy-hog are all local names for what kind of animal?

11. Where do herons build their nests?

12. Where would you expect to find a bladderwort?

13. What is ichthyology?

14. How many woodpecker species breed in Britain?

15. What does the name dinosaur actually mean?

16. What colour is the celandine flower?

17. What is a feral creature?

18. Why do farmers not like barberry bushes in their hedges?

19. What is the more familiar name of the great maple?

20. What name is given to a male giraffe?

1 A tidal wave or wall of water, up to 2.7 m (9 ft) high, that rushes up the lower reaches of the River Severn at the time of the highest tides

2 A vulture: it is also known as the bearded vulture

3 South America

4 The sedge family or Cyperaceae

5 A marine crustacean related to the woodlice: it bores into submerged timber and causes damage to groynes and harbour installations

6 The peregrine falcon, which is up to 48 cm (19 in) long. The gyrfalcon is a little larger, but it is only a rare visitor to Britain

7 True: the platypus and the echidna are egg-laying mammals

8 Sand eels

9 A plant that lives for several or many years

10 The woodlouse

11 Usually in the tree tops

12 In still or slow-moving water: it is an insectivorous plant

13 The study of fishes

14 Three – the green, great spotted and lesser spotted woodpeckers

15 Terrible lizard

16 Yellow – this is true of both lesser and greater celandine

17 Any animal now living wild but descended from domesticated stock. The town or feral pigeon is a good example, and there are also many feral cats in our towns

18 Because barberry leaves harbour rust fungi that can spread to wheat crops

19 The sycamore

20 A bull

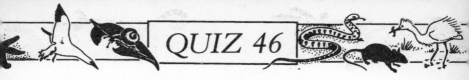

QUIZ 46

1 Which is the world's biggest desert?

2 What is a black-veined white?

3 What is the more common name of the quickthorn?

4 What month traditionally comes in like a lion and goes out like a lamb?

5 How many living rhinoceros species are there?

6 What name is given to a young goose?

7 What is hydroponics?

8 Garden fertiliser packets normally indicate the amount of N, P and K that they contain: what do these letters stand for?

9 Why are mountain animals often darker than their lowland relatives?

10 What is a wisent?

11 How would you distinguish a half-grown newt tadpole from frog and toad tadpoles?

12 What do the letters CITES stand for in the field of nature conservation?

13 What colour are the flowers of the common toadflax?

14 What kind of plant is Irish moss or carrageen?

15 What do we call the process by which streams and other natural agencies wear away the earth's surface?

16 What is a loquat?

17 What insects can be leaf, bark, or ground?

18 Where do arboreal animals live?

19 What is royal jelly?

20 Name the largest of the marsupials

1 The Sahara, which stretches over 4,800 km (3,000 miles) across the northern half of Africa from the Atlantic to the Red Sea. Covering about 8,320,000 km² (3,250,000 miles²), it is bigger than all the other deserts put together

2 A butterfly

3 The hawthorn

4 March

5 Five – Indian, Javan, Sumatran, Black and White

6 A gosling

7 The soilless culture of crops or other plants. The plants are grown in solutions containing all the necessary minerals

8 Nitrogen, phosphorus and potassium

9 Because dark colours absorb the sun's radiant heat more efficiently, so it is useful to have a dark coat in the cold mountain air

10 It is the alternative name of the European bison

11 Newt tadpoles retain their external gills

12 Convention on International Trade in Endangered Species – an international agreement designed to protect rare species by regulating or prohibiting trade in them

13 Yellow

14 It is a red seaweed

15 Erosion

16 The fruit of a small evergreen tree belonging to the rose family

17 Beetles

18 In trees

19 An oily, protein-rich secretion of honey bees that is given to the bee grubs

20 The great grey kangaroo or the red kangaroo, both of which can grow to a height of about 2 metres (6 ft 6 in)

QUIZ 47

1 What does a mycologist study?

2 What happens to a black-headed gull's head in the autumn?

3 What kind of animal is a black molly?

4 What is the main difference between the tail flukes or fins of a whale and those of a fish?

5 What does the hornet use to build its nest?

6 The bolas spider catches moths by whirling a single thread of silk with a blob of glue on the end: true or false?

7 What colour are the petals of borage flowers?

8 Which gas do plants take in and use during photosynthesis?

9 What does the damage to our clothes – the clothes moth or its caterpillar?

10 What is the main food of frugivorous birds?

11 Where would you find a pair of elytra?

12 The caves at Lascaux in France are world famous: for what?

13 What is a pratincole?

14 A soft, juicy fruit with numerous seeds embedded in the flesh is a definition of what kind of fruit?

15 Which is the world's largest seal?

16 What plants can be black, woody, or deadly?

17 Which is Britain's largest national park?

18 What is the bole of a tree?

19 To what family of butterflies do the coppers and hairstreaks belong?

20 What kind of habitat is a carr?

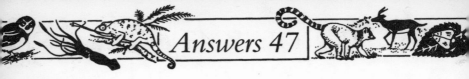

1 Fungi

2 It turns white, except for a small dark smudge behind the eye

3 A tropical fish, related to the guppy and very popular in aquaria

4 The whale flukes are horizontal and the fish flukes are vertical

5 Paper, made from dead wood that the insects chew into pulp

6 True: the glue or gum smells like a female moth and the males are attracted to it

7 Blue

8 Carbon dioxide

9 The caterpillar: the adults do not feed at all

10 Fruit

11 On a beetle: the elytra are the tough front wings

12 Prehistoric cave paintings, depicting a variety of animals

13 A bird

14 A berry

15 The elephant seal, males of which reach lengths of about 6 m (20 ft) and weigh up to 3650 kg (8000 lb)

16 Nightshades

17 The Lake District National Park, with an area of about 225,000 hectares (870 miles^2)

18 The trunk

19 The Lycaenidae or blue family

20 A damp woodland, often dominated by sallow and alder scrub and usually a stage in the development of woodland from a fen or a marsh (accept fenland)

QUIZ 48

1 What is the common name for a cat's vibrissae?

2 What is the more familiar name for the animal sometimes known as a cavy?

3 Raft, house and trapdoor are examples of which large group of animals?

4 What are the principal flowers in the family Campanulaceae?

5 To what family does the jackal belong?

6 What proportion of the earth's surface is covered with water?

7 What name is given to a young swan?

8 Blakeney, famous for its seal colonies, is on the coast of which English county?

9 What kind of animal was an ichthyosaur?

10 Constricting snakes have no venom, so how do they kill their prey?

11 With what do tailor birds make their nests?

12 What name is given to the upper part of a tortoise's shell and also to the upper part of a crab's shell?

13 What colour are the legs of a redshank?

14 What gas is given out when plants make food by photosynthesis?

15 What is a tarn?

16 Where would you find annual rings?

17 According to legend, how did the robin get its red breast?

18 Many Scottish place names contain the word strath: what does strath mean?

19 What early-flowering garden plant is scientifically called *Galanthus nivalis*?

20 What is the opposite of nocturnal?

1 Whiskers

2 The guinea pig

3 Spiders

4 Bellflowers

5 The dog family or Canidae

6 70% (accept anything between 65% and 75% inclusive)

7 A cygnet

8 Norfolk

9 A marine reptile, very like a dolphin in shape, that was alive during the age of the dinosaurs but died out over 100 million years ago

10 They wrap their bodies around their victims and squeeze them until they suffocate: they do not actually crush them

11 With leaves, sewn together with fine roots and other fibres, including silk from spider webs. The bird uses its beak as a needle

12 The carapace

13 Red

14 Oxygen

15 A small lake or pool, especially in upland regions

16 In a tree trunk

17 By pulling the thorns from Christ's crown of thorns

18 Valley

19 The snowdrop

20 Diurnal

QUIZ 49

1 What do stoats, arctic foxes and ptarmigans have in common?

2 What do cecidologists study?

3 What period of the earth's history came between the Silurian and Carboniferous periods?

4 What kind of animal is a black widow?

5 Which group of birds includes species called rockhopper, macaroni and chinstrap?

6 The king cobra, up to 5 m long, is the longest poisonous snake: what does it eat?

7 To which continent would you go to explore the Pampas?

8 What kinds of plants belong to the group known as bryophytes?

9 What is the more common name of the mavis?

10 What colour are the flowers of black nightshade?

11 What is a yellow-stainer?

12 What do sealions and fur seals have that true seals, such as the grey seal, do not have?

13 How would you distinguish between a mute swan and a whooper swan?

14 How did the African secretary bird get its name?

15 The loofah, with which you might scrub your back in the bath, is the fibrous skeleton of a kind of marrow: true or false?

16 What is or was a quagga?

17 Boston ivy covers the walls of thousands of houses all over Britain, but where did this vigorous climbing plant originate?

18 What are wainscots, prominents and lutestrings?

19 Where do skylarks make their nests?

20 What is the emblem of the Worldwide Fund for Nature?

1 They can all turn white for the winter

2 Plant galls

3 The Devonian Period

4 A very poisonous spider

5 Penguins

6 Other snakes

7 South America: Pampas is the name given to the extensive grasslands

8 Mosses and liverworts

9 Song thrush

10 White: the fruits are black

11 A kind of mushroom, named for the way in which its flesh turns bright yellow when broken. It can cause unpleasant digestive upsets, although these are usually only temporary

12 External ears, or ear-flaps

13 The mute swan has an orange bill but the whooper swan's bill is largely yellow

14 Because the long, black-tipped feathers on its head resemble the old-fashioned quill pens that clerks used to stick behind their ears or into their wigs

15 True

16 It was a zebra-like animal that lived in South Africa and became extinct in 1884

17 China, Japan and other parts of eastern Asia

18 Moths

19 On the ground

20 The giant panda

QUIZ 50

1 What starts on the Glorious Twelfth (of August)?

2 What sort of fruit is a drupe?

3 What do we call the thick layer of fat under the skin of seals and whales?

4 What is a sidewinder?

5 What kinds of animals include species called brain, stagshorn and cup?

6 How does the gladiator spider catch its prey?

7 What is the proper name of the vast coniferous forest belt stretching right across the Northern Hemisphere and covering much of Scandinavia, Siberia and Canada?

8 Which is the odd one out: ringed seal, harp seal, leopard seal and grey seal?

9 What do the monarch butterflies of North America do in the autumn?

10 Which animals forage in groups called sounders?

11 Wallace's Line marks the boundary between the Oriental and Australasian faunas: through which country does it pass?

12 Which plant family is characterised by the domed or umbrella-shaped flowerheads known as umbels?

13 Which is the largest of the flatfishes?

14 What colour are the flowers of the Welsh poppy?

15 What is the fundamental difference between a bulb and a corm?

16 What name is given to the earliest known bird?

17 Name the biologist who first discovered the dances of honey bees

18 What are dabberlocks?

19 The giraffe's neck contains the same number of bones as that of a man: true or false?

20 Water tiger is the name given to the larva of what kind of insect?

1 The grouse-shooting season

2 A stone-fruit – one whose seed is enclosed in a woody pip or 'stone', which is in turn embedded in the flesh. Plums, peaches and cherries are familiar examples

3 Blubber

4 A desert-dwelling rattlesnake, named for its sideways movement across the sand (accept snake)

5 Corals

6 It throws its web at its prey, which gets thoroughly tangled up in it

7 The taiga

8 The leopard seal: it lives in the Antarctic, but the others live in the northern hemisphere

9 They fly south to hibernate in Mexico, California and Florida

10 Wild boar and swans (accept pigs)

11 Indonesia

12 The carrot family or Apiaceae (accept Umbelliferae, which is the older name for the family, and also parsley family)

13 The halibut, which can reach a length of 4 m (13 ft) and a weight of about 300 kg (660 lb)

14 Yellow

15 A bulb stores its food in clusters of juicy scales or leaf bases, but a corm stores its food in a short, rounded stem

16 *Archaeopteryx*

17 Karl von Frisch

18 Large brown seaweeds

19 True: there are seven neck bones or cervical vertebrae in all mammals

20 The diving beetle *(Dytiscus)*, which is a fierce predator in both young and adult stages

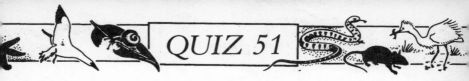

QUIZ 51

1 What does it mean if an insect is described as apterous?

2 What do we normally call a seal colony?

3 What is a coyote?

4 Why do snakes continually flick out their tongues?

5 With what do weaver ants make their nests?

6 From what animal do we get the reddish brown pigment known as sepia?

7 Where would you be most likely to find alder trees?

8 What is an echidna?

9 How does the tumbleweed scatter its seeds?

10 What colour is the crown of a male English house sparrow?

11 What group of flowers includes species called Welsh, Arctic and long-headed?

12 What proportion of the earth's atmosphere is composed of oxygen?

13 From what kinds of animals do we get natural pearls?

14 What is the alternative common name of the policeman's helmet flower?

15 Peas, beans and their relatives are collectively known as legumes: to which family do they belong?

16 What are the most famous inhabitants of Aldabra Island?

17 A group of geese on the ground is called a gaggle, but what do we call a group of geese in flight?

18 What sort of animal is a noctule?

19 What is a spring squill?

20 What word do we use to refer to all the chemical processes that go on in a living body?

1 It is wingless

2 A rookery

3 A dog-like animal, closely related to the wolf, living in North America. It is also called the prairie wolf

4 To smell things: the tongue picks up scent particles from the air or the ground and helps the snake to find prey

5 Leaves, glued together with sticky silk produced by the ant grubs

6 The cuttlefish, whose scientific name is *Sepia*

7 On river banks or in damp woodlands

8 It is a spiny egg-laying mammal of Australia, also known as the spiny anteater

9 The mature plant snaps off at the base and it rolls around in the wind, dropping its seeds as it goes

10 Grey

11 Poppies

12 21%

13 Oysters and mussels

14 Indian balsam

15 The Fabaceae (accept Leguminosae and Papilionaceae, which are older names for the family)

16 Giant tortoises

17 A skein

18 A bat

19 A flower, related to the bluebell and usually found on coastal grassland

20 Metabolism

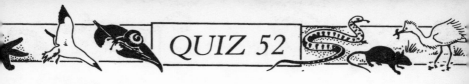

QUIZ 52

1 What is anthropology?

2 Name the world's largest antelope

3 For what bird do people in northern Europe often erect nesting platforms on their houses?

4 What is a barracuda?

5 The River Thames rises in the Cheviot Hills: true or false?

6 According to a well-known proverb, what gets the worm?

7 For what do we use extracts from pyrethrum flowers?

8 What animals can be brown, striped, or spotted?

9 What colour is a female blackbird?

10 What is a tawny grisette?

11 What part of a flower receives the pollen when the flower is pollinated?

12 What is the easiest way to distinguish a grasshopper from a cricket on sight?

13 Where is the Kalahari Desert?

14 Sandgrouse nest in extremely dry places and fly many miles every day to collect water for their nestlings. How do they carry the water back to their nests?

15 What name is commonly given to beech nuts?

16 Most land snails and many freshwater snails belong to the group called pulmonates: what does this word mean?

17 How many toes does a rhinoceros have?

18 *Saintpaulia* is a popular house plant: what is its more familiar name?

19 How are the seeds of willowherbs scattered?

20 To which family of birds does the canary belong?

1 The study of human evolution and culture

2 The eland, which can stand nearly 2 m (6 ft 6 in) at the shoulder

3 The white stork

4 A fast-moving marine predatory fish armed with fearsome teeth

5 False: it rises in the Cotswold Hills

6 The early bird

7 As an insecticide

8 Hyaenas

9 Brown

10 A fungus

11 The stigma

12 Grasshopper antennae are shorter than the body: cricket antennae are longer than the body

13 In southern Africa, occupying parts of Namibia, Botswana and South Africa

14 In their feathers, which soak up the water like a sponge

15 Beech mast

16 With lungs

17 Twelve – three on each foot, although the weight is borne on just the central toe of each foot

18 The African violet

19 They are very fluffy and they are scattered by the wind

20 The finch family or *Fringillidae*

QUIZ 53

1 What does a limnologist study?

2 Which is the smallest British bird?

3 What is viper's bugloss?

4 To which order of mammals does the kinkajou belong?

5 Some slugs chase earthworms through their tunnels and eat them: true or false?

6 What animals include breeds called Exmoor, Dartmoor and New Forest?

7 What do we call the edible part of a potato plant?

8 In the natural world, what are lawyers' wigs?

9 How did the lobster moth get its name?

10 What the are Somerset Levels?

11 These black and white cattle are called Holsteins in America: what do we call them in Britain?

12 What do the initials FOE stand for in the field of conservation?

13 What is a bandicoot?

14 What is lignum vitae?

15 What is the more familiar name of the house plant whose scientific name is *Ficus elastica*?

16 What happens to a wood when it is coppiced?

17 What do we call inherited behaviour patterns that enable animals to catch food and carry out other activities without ever having to learn?

18 What colour is the female chalkhill blue butterfly?

19 What do we call the flower clusters of willow and poplar trees?

20 What crop has been turning huge areas of Britain yellow during the spring in recent years?

1 Ponds and streams and their wildlife (accept freshwater)

2 The goldcrest or the firecrest, both of which are only about 9 cm (3 in) long

3 A wild flower, related to the forget-me-not, with bristly leaves and blue petals

4 The Carnivora or carnivorous mammals

5 True

6 Ponies (accept horses)

7 A tuber

8 Fungi, also called shaggy ink-caps

9 From its unusual caterpillar, which has long, slender front legs that wave about like lobster antennae

10 An area of low-lying marsh and peat bog between the Mendips and the Quantock Hills

11 Friesians

12 Friends of the Earth

13 An Australian marsupial mammal

14 A tropical tree of the genus *Guaiacum* or the heavy, oily timber from it

15 The rubber plant

16 All or most of the trees are cut to ground level and left to send up new shoots or poles. This system of woodland management has long been used to produce timber for hurdles, fencing and firewood

17 Instincts

18 Brown

19 Catkins

20 Oil-seed rape

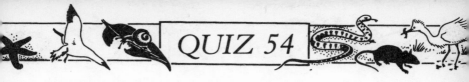

QUIZ 54

1 What birds belong to the family Corvidae?

2 What grass is always included in seed mixtures intended for producing hard-wearing lawns?

3 What is a boll weevil?

4 Who wrote *The Compleat Angler*?

5 A sultana is a dried what?

6 What would you measure with an anemometer?

7 What does a malacologist study?

8 What is the more common name for the painful condition called urticaria?

9 What are fossorial animals?

10 What is a grey dagger?

11 Which is the odd one out: dace, whiting, plaice, sole?

12 How many wings has a wasp?

13 Could you find gorse in flower on New Year's Day?

14 What is the name of the hot, dry wind that blows up from North Africa and often carries dust from the Sahara across the Mediterranean Sea to Europe?

15 The male of which duck has white flanks and a drooping crest at the back of its head?

16 What are ratites?

17 Name Britain's largest land snail

18 What insect used to be called the 'hop-dog'?

19 What, in the world of plants, is a lady's slipper?

20 What is a dik-dik?

1 Crows (accept jays, jackdaws, rooks and magpies)

2 Rye grass

3 A beetle whose grubs feed in the developing cotton heads (bolls) and seriously reduce the cotton crop

4 Izaak Walton

5 Grape

6 Wind speed

7 Molluscs (accept slugs and snails)

8 Nettle rash

9 Digging or burrowing animals

10 A moth

11 The dace: it is a freshwater fish and the others live in the sea

12 Four

13 Yes: gorse flowers at any time of the year, although the flowers are most abundant in early spring

14 The sirocco

15 The tufted duck

16 Large flightless birds, including the ostrich and the emu

17 The Roman snail, also known as the edible snail

18 The caterpillar of the pale tussock moth, which used to be very common in the hop fields: its hair tufts used to cause much irritation to the skin of the hop-pickers

19 An orchid

20 A small African antelope

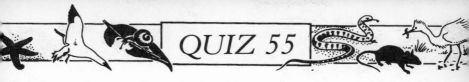

QUIZ 55

1 What do we call the form of camouflage in which the lower side of an animal's body is paler than its back, thus helping to cancel out the shadows on the lower part of the body?

2 What is a nilghai?

3 Why do walruses go pink when lying on the seashore?

4 What are the Everglades?

5 Which rare bird has had its nest site at Loch Garten in Scotland closely guarded by bird-watchers for many years?

6 What is the difference between a shaddock and a shanny?

7 Which seabird has the scientific name *Puffinus puffinus*?

8 What is a galah?

9 What is krill?

10 Does the gladiolus grow from a bulb or from a corm?

11 In what field of biology did Konrad Lorenz become famous?

12 Which animal group has members called edible, marsh and paradoxical?

13 What is batology?

14 Which bird is also known as the solan goose?

15 What name is given to the mating season of deer?

16 What is peat made from?

17 The government-funded body responsible for the conservation of wildlife and the environment in England is now called English Nature. What was it called before 1991?

18 What is a Portuguese man-o'-war?

19 What are diatoms?

20 These birds are called loons in America: what do we call them in Britain?

1 Countershading

2 A large Indian antelope, sometimes called a blue bull

3 Because the blood vessels in the skin enlarge and carry more blood close to the surface, in just the same way that we go red when we get hot

4 An area of marsh and swamp in Florida, covering about 13,000 km² (5000 miles²) and supporting a wide variety of sub-tropical flora and fauna. Part of the area is contained in the Everglades National Park

5 The osprey

6 A shaddock is a citrus fruit, rather like a grapefruit, but a shanny is a fish belonging to the blenny family

7 The Manx shearwater

8 An Australian cockatoo, famous for its pink plumage (accept bird)

9 A planktonic, shrimp-like crustacean which forms the bulk of the food of the blue whale and other whalebone whales (accept plankton)

10 A corm

11 The field of animal behaviour or ethology

12 Frogs

13 The study of brambles, of which there are hundreds of different forms or micro-species in Britain

14 The gannet

15 The rut or rutting season

16 Partly decayed vegetation, especially bog mosses

17 The Nature Conservancy Council

18 A floating marine animal, often called a jellyfish, although it is not a true jellyfish

19 Microscopic, single-celled algae, usually with box-like glassy shells made of silica. Most live in the sea or in fresh water

20 Divers

QUIZ 56

1 If pathology is the study of diseases, what is phytopathology?

2 What is the alternative name of the gnu?

3 What name is given to the annual tradition of catching and marking the swans on the River Thames?

4 What is a copperhead?

5 Where might you find a cassowary living in the wild?

6 Apart from the difference in size, how would you most easily distinguish a common prawn from a common shrimp?

7 Before cotton was available in Europe, the fibres from stinging nettle stems were used to make cloth: true or false?

8 What colour are gorse flowers?

9 What is a predatory animal?

10 What is the main food of the osprey?

11 Which animals have the most legs?

12 What is wrong with the following observation? 'I watched the grass snake slither across the roadside verge, grab a frog and swallow it whole. The snake then curled up in a sunny spot at the base of the hedge, closed its eyes, and went to sleep. A bulge slowly moving along its body marked the position of the unfortunate frog.'

13 What name is often given to an eagle's nest?

14 What is a porbeagle?

15 What are the principal birds in the family Phasianidae?

16 What colour is the crown of a female blackcap?

17 What popular garden fruit is a cross between a blackberry and a raspberry?

18 What is a rill?

19 What low-growing plants, often cultivated in gardens, include species called purple, yellow and mossy?

20 What British bird spits an oily liquid at anyone approaching its nest?

1 The study of plant diseases

2 The wildebeeste

3 Swan-upping

4 A snake

5 In New Guinea or in Northern Australia

6 The prawn has a toothed 'spear' or rostrum on the top of its head

7 True

8 Yellow

9 Any animal that hunts other species for food

10 Fish

11 Millipedes: some species have more than 700 legs

12 Snakes have no eyelids and thus cannot close their eyes

13 An eyrie or aerie

14 A kind of shark

15 Pheasants

16 Brown

17 The loganberry, named after James Logan, the American horticulturalist (and judge) who first developed it

18 A small stream

19 Saxifrages

20 The fulmar

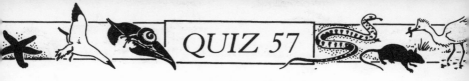

QUIZ 57

1 Which is the most abundant bird in the world?

2 How do grasshoppers sing?

3 To what does the word edaphic refer?

4 What sort of animal is a monitor?

5 The Scots call it a bluebell, but what is it called in England?

6 What happens to a tree when it is pollarded?

7 Stone and spined are the two British species of which kind of fish?

8 What is arachnophobia?

9 What are the two main colours of wild budgerigars?

10 What is the more familiar name of Indian corn?

11 What name is given to the group of animals that chew the cud?

12 What is the more common name of nacre, the smooth material lining the insides of many sea-shells?

13 Where did the passenger pigeon live until it was shot to extinction early in the 20th century?

14 What birds use their beaks like fishing nets?

15 What do we call plants that store water in fleshy leaves or stems?

16 What colour is the head of a male reed bunting?

17 What nickname was given to Lancelot Brown – a famous 18th century gardener?

18 What animals are described as equine?

19 In which English county is the bulk of Exmoor National Park?

20 Which is the odd one out: marrow, melon, tomato, cucumber?

1 The domestic chicken: no accurate figures are available, but it is estimated that there are well over 4,000 million chickens in the world

2 By rubbing their back legs against their wings: a row of tiny pegs on each leg is drawn over a hard vein on the wing and this causes the vibrations that we hear as sounds

3 The soil

4 A lizard

5 The harebell

6 It is periodically lopped at a height of about 3 m. New branches grow at this level. This method of timber production was widely used in forests where deer were common, to prevent the deer from browsing on the new shoots

7 Loach

8 The fear of spiders

9 Green and yellow

10 Maize

11 Ruminants

12 Mother-of-pearl

13 North America

14 Pelicans

15 Succulents

16 Black

17 Capability

18 Horses and their relatives in the family Equidae

19 Somerset

20 The tomato: it belongs to the potato family, but the others are all members of the squash family – the Cucurbitaceae

QUIZ 58

1 What is chlorosis?

2 What group of insects includes species called German, American and common?

3 On what kinds of soil would you find calcicole plants?

4 Which butterfly became extinct in England in 1975, although it continues to flourish in the west of Scotland?

5 Apart from being mammals, what do fox, goat and leopard have in common?

6 What do we call the region of the sea bed that slopes gently down from the shore to a depth of about 200 m?

7 London stands at one end of the ancient road known as Ermine Street, but what city stands at the other end?

8 What sort of mammal is a muntjac?

9 By what other name do we know the plant called totters?

10 What does the word caespitose (sess–pit–owes) mean when applied to a plant?

11 What organisms cause mosaic disease in potatoes and various other plants?

12 What are cutworms?

13 What are the two main colours of fritillary butterflies?

14 On a map, what are isohyets?

15 What is a butcher's broom?

16 If a leaf is described as spatulate, what is its shape?

17 What are dehiscent fruits?

18 What is the alternative name of the large beetle often called a may-bug?

19 Good King Henry, now found mainly on waste ground, was once cultivated and eaten like spinach: true or false?

20 What is generally regarded as the world's most venomous fish?

1 A deficiency of chlorophyll in a plant, causing the leaves to become pale green or yellow

2 Cockroaches

3 Chalky or other lime-rich soils

4 The chequered skipper

5 They are also the names of moths

6 The continental shelf

7 York

8 It is a small deer

9 Quaking grass

10 Tufted or growing in dense tufts

11 Viruses

12 The caterpillars of certain moths, so called because they chew right through plant stems at ground level

13 Orange and black (accept orange and brown, for some markings are dark brown)

14 Lines joining places with equal rainfall

15 A shrubby plant related to the lily family

16 Spoon-shaped

17 Fruits that split open to release their seeds

18 The cockchafer

19 True

20 The stonefish, several species of which live in the Red Sea and in coastal waters of the Indo-Pacific region

QUIZ 59

1 What is a honeyguide on a flower?

2 What sort of animal is a honeyguide?

3 Where would you find a stalactite?

4 Which order of insects has the greatest number of known species?

5 What do the letters RHS stand for in connection with plants?

6 What collective name is sometimes applied to a group of mules?

7 Which common British bird buries acorns in the autumn?

8 What kind of animal is a zander?

9 What colour are the flowers of the periwinkle?

10 Modern plant family names all end in which five letters?

11 Which is the odd one out: barnacle, shrimp, mussel, crab?

12 What is an animal's spoor?

13 What have these hedgerow plants in common: honeysuckle, traveller's joy, bramble, cleavers?

14 Which vegetable is said to help you to see in the dark?

15 What is charlock?

16 What is an atoll?

17 Black swans are native to what part of the world?

18 What insects can be assassins or damsels?

19 What sort of animal is a yak?

20 All moths fly at night: true or false?

1 It is a line or other pattern guiding bees to the nectar

2 A bird

3 In a cave: it is a column of limestone hanging from the roof rather like an icicle

4 The Coleoptera or beetles

5 Royal Horticultural Society

6 A pack or a clan

7 The jay

8 A fish

9 Blue or violet

10 –aceae

11 The mussel: it is a mollusc and the others are all crustaceans

12 Its footprint or track

13 They are all climbers

14 The carrot – because its carotene is converted to vitamin A, which is known to be necessary for the efficient working of the eyes

15 A weed or wild plant with yellow flowers and rather bristly stems and leaves. A member of the cabbage family, it is common in arable fields and waste places

16 A coral island, usually circular with a lagoon in the centre

17 Australia

18 Bugs

19 A kind of cattle from the Himalayas, where it is domesticated and used for many purposes

20 False

QUIZ 60

1 What is a guanaco (gwah–nar–coe)?

2 Which is the odd one out: smolt, parr, roach, grilse?

3 Why is the grapefruit so called?

4 In which part of the world would you be if you were watching birds of paradise flying in the wild?

5 How does the brown pelican get its food?

6 What birds can be spruce, hazel, or willow?

7 Where are a garden snail's eyes?

8 What kind of animal is a skink?

9 Steller's and Californian are two species of what?

10 What is the main food of the hippopotamus?

11 What is the common name of the cat with the scientific name *Acinonyx jubatus*?

12 When did Kew Gardens celebrate its 150th anniversary, which was marked by the issue of a set of four postage stamps: 1970, 1980, or 1990?

13 In which English county is the New Forest?

14 What sort of animal is a flying fox?

15 What, in connection with the weather, is precipitation?

16 What have vapourer, winter and mottled umber moths in common?

17 What name do we usually give to a female sheep?

18 Many English place names contain wald or weald: what does this mean?

19 What is the more common name of the flowers sometimes known as hardheads?

20 What are passerines?

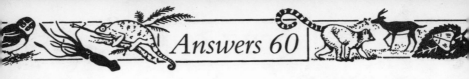

1 A South American mammal belonging to the camel family

2 The roach: the others are all stages in the development of the salmon

3 Because the wild form is quite small and grows in bunches like grapes

4 New Guinea and neighbouring parts of South-east Asia and northern Australia

5 It dives into the sea from the air, unlike the white pelicans which fish from the surface

6 Grouse

7 At the tips of its tentacles

8 A lizard

9 Sea lions

10 Grass and other vegetation, usually gathered on land at night

11 The cheetah

12 1990

13 Hampshire

14 A bat: the name is given to several of the larger fruit-eating bats, whose faces are very fox-like

15 Rain, snow, sleet, or hail – anything that falls from the clouds (accept dew, which is also regarded as a form of precipitation)

16 They all have wingless females

17 A ewe

18 Wood or forest

19 Knapweeds

20 Song-birds or perching birds: any birds belonging to the order Passeriformes, which is the largest of all the bird groups

1 What does an exobiologist do?

2 On which continent would you find wild rheas?

3 What is unusual about the larvae of many caddis flies?

4 Which cuckoo makes the familiar call of 'cuck-coo' – the male or the female?

5 What are setters, pointers, and boxers?

6 Insect eyes often contain thousands of tiny lenses. What are these lenses called?

7 ICBP is the world's oldest international conservation organisation. What do the letters stand for?

8 What sort of animal is a francolin?

9 In the world of plants, what are pneumatophores (new–mat–oh–fours)?

10 The animal kingdom is divided into about thirty major groups called ... What is the missing word?

11 What is plankton?

12 What kind of insect is a wart-biter?

13 What do we call the red flap hanging from a turkey's neck?

14 Apart from its tusks, how many teeth does a mature elephant have in use at any one time?

15 What sort of animal is a stargazer?

16 Why do vultures have bald heads?

17 What are podsols, rendzinas, and brown earths?

18 The first jeans were made from hemp fibres – from the same kind of plant that yields marijuana: true or false?

19 What name is used for a male rabbit?

20 Name the two kinds of bryony that climb in our hedgerows

1 Search for extra-terrestrial life or life on other planets

2 South America

3 They build portable cases with grains of sand and vegetable debris

4 The male

5 Breeds of dog

6 Facets

7 International Council for Bird Preservation

8 A bird belonging to the pheasant family, with many species in Africa and Asia

9 Breathing roots, characteristic of mangroves and other swamp plants: they stick up through the mud or water and absorb air

10 Phyla (accept phylum, which is the singular form)

11 The small plant and animal life that drifts in the surface layers of seas and lakes

12 A bush-cricket (accept cricket, but not grasshopper)

13 The wattle

14 Four – one on each side of each jaw

15 A fish that lives on the seabed and is named because its eyes look straight up

16 Because their feathers would get caked with blood and would be very hard to clean after plunging their heads into carcasses

17 Kinds of soil

18 True

19 A buck

20 White bryony and black bryony, which are not at all related

QUIZ 62

1 What name is given to a female tiger?

2 What is palaeogeography (pal-ee-oh-geography)?

3 Would you find bracken on acidic soils or alkaline ones?

4 What colour is the face of a goldfinch?

5 What is a bird's syrinx?

6 What birds can be scarlet, glossy, or bald?

7 What is a nyala?

8 In what sort of habitat would you look for Apollo butterflies?

9 To what family do the world's tallest flowering trees belong?

10 What general name is given to dugongs and manatees?

11 Which is the smallest native British deer?

12 What are Timothy, Yorkshire fog, and barren brome?

13 What is a blanket bog?

14 Where are a cricket's ears?

15 How did the nuthatch get its name?

16 What is a lily-trotter?

17 From what kinds of organisms do we get litmus, used as an indicator to determine whether liquids are acidic or alkaline?

18 What are the principal plants in the family Ranunculaceae?

19 What is a stag-headed tree?

20 What is the collective name for a group of partridges?

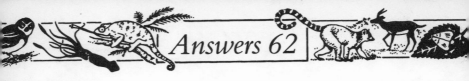

1 Tigress

2 The study of the geographical features of prehistoric times

3 Acidic

4 Red

5 Its voice-box – the equivalent of the mammalian larynx

6 Ibises

7 An African antelope

8 Mountains or mountainous regions

9 The eucalyptus family or Myrtaceae (accept gum-tree family). Some eucalyptus or gum trees are over 100 m (330 ft) tall, and one cut down some years ago was reported as being over 130 m (435 ft) tall – taller than any living conifer.

10 Sea cows

11 The roe deer

12 Grasses

13 An extensive peat bog covering many upland areas of northern and western Britain. It occurs in cool areas with high rainfall and low evaporation and the peat can be many feet thick

14 On its front legs, close to the 'knee joints'

15 Because it wedges nuts into bark crevices and hammers them open with its bill

16 A long-toed water bird, named for its habit of walking over floating vegetation. It is also called a jacana

17 Lichens

18 Buttercups (accept crowfoots)

19 A tree with dead upper branches that resemble a stag's antlers. This dying back of the upper branches is quite natural in old oaks and some other trees

20 A covey

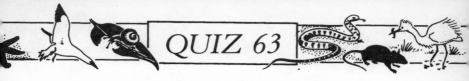

QUIZ 63

1 What does an ethologist study?

2 What is the main food of the polar bear?

3 In what kind of rock do flints develop?

4 What do colobus, langur, mangabey, and macaque all have in common?

5 What is the difference between a potto and a potoo?

6 What bird smashes bones by dropping them on to rocks?

7 'The study of the relationships between plants and animals and their environment' is a definition of which branch of biology?

8 What is a gila monster?

9 How can you most easily separate vetches (*Vicia* species) from the various species of wild peas and vetchlings (*Lathyrus* species)?

10 What is a limestone pavement?

11 What name is given to the larva of a butterfly or a moth?

12 By what name do we know the flying reptiles that flourished during the time of the dinosaurs?

13 What is a Peruvian apple or love apple?

14 What kind of bird is a yaffle?

15 What kind of plant is papyrus, from which the ancient Egyptians made paper?

16 What is a saltmarsh?

17 Where did clothes moths and other fabric pests live before we had houses full of clothes and carpets for them to nibble?

18 Which is the odd one out: haddock, perch, carp, pike?

19 What colour are the ripe fruits of the white bryony?

20 Who wrote the poem called *To Autumn*, the first line of which is 'Season of mists and mellow fruitfulness!'?

1 Animal behaviour

2 Seals

3 Chalk

4 They are all kinds of monkeys

5 A potto is a small African mammal related to the bushbabies, while a potoo is an American bird related to the nightjars

6 The lammergeier or bearded vulture, which then eats the shattered bones

7 Ecology

8 A venomous lizard from the deserts of North America

9 Vetches have smoothly rounded stems; peas and vetchlings have flanged or winged stems

10 A more or less bare horizontal outcrop of limestone rock, scraped clear of soil by the ice age glaciers and then dissected into blocks by the rainwater running over the surface

11 A caterpillar

12 Pterosaurs, meaning winged lizards (accept pterodactyls, although these were just one particular group of pterosaurs)

13 A tomato

14 It is another name for the green woodpecker

15 A sedge

16 A marsh fringing the sea or an estuary that is periodically flooded by the tide, and therefore very salty and colonised only by salt-tolerant plants

17 In the nests of birds and rodents, where they fed on feathers and hair

18 Haddock: it is a marine fish and the others live in freshwater

19 Red

20 John Keats

QUIZ 64

1 What collective name is sometimes used for a group of cats?

2 Which thrush is seen in Britain only as a summer visitor?

3 What is the difference between a stalactite and a stalagmite?

4 Where would you find a turnstone?

5 What is topiary?

6 What sort of animal is a drongo?

7 Which is the odd one out: orchid, crocus, geranium, lily, iris?

8 What colour is a rook's beak?

9 How does cleavers or goosegrass cling to the surrounding vegetation as it climbs?

10 Which order of mammals do apes, monkeys, and humans belong to?

11 What is set-aside?

12 What is the main food of a marabou?

13 What covered much of Europe during Pleistocene times?

14 Where are a mammal's incisor teeth?

15 What is correct name for the plant commonly known as old-man's-beard?

16 What is a backswimmer?

17 What seabirds do Chinese and Japanese fishermen sometimes train to catch fish?

18 What colour are chicory flowers?

19 In the classification of animals, what rank comes between a phylum and an order?

20 What is the national flower of Wales?

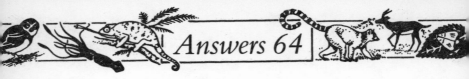

1 A clouder or a clutter

2 The ring ouzel

3 A stalactite grows down from the roof of a cave and a stalagmite grows up from the floor: both are made of limestone deposited from running water

4 Most likely on the seashore: it is a small wading bird

5 The art of clipping hedges and shrubs into decorative shapes – especially into the shapes of animals

6 A bird, with a long and often forked tail

7 Geranium: it is a dicotyledon with rounded leaves, but the others are all monocotyledons with slender or spear-shaped leaves

8 Grey

9 Tiny hooks on its leaves and stems catch on the other plants

10 The primates

11 Agricultural land that has been temporarily taken out of production

12 Carrion: it is an African stork that feeds by scavenging, often clearing up the remains of lions' kills in the company of vultures

13 Ice or glaciers

14 At the front of the mouth

15 Traveller's-joy (accept clematis)

16 An aquatic bug

17 Cormorants: the birds are fitted with fairly tight collars that prevent them from swallowing the fish, but the collars are periodically loosened and the birds are given a fish as a reward

18 Blue

19 A class

20 The daffodil

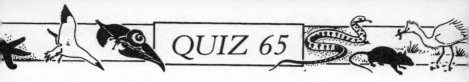

QUIZ 65

1 What is ethnobotany?

2 What shape are the buds of the European beech tree?

3 What are pintails, harlequins and shovelers?

4 Approximately how many spines does the average adult hedgehog have: about 3000, about 5000, or about 15,000?

5 What sort of animal is an ani?

6 In what part of the world are the open grasslands known as the Veldt?

7 From what kind of plant do we get rattan, which provides most of the cane used for wickerwork?

8 What is a john dory?

9 When is the closed season for coarse fishing in British rivers?

10 How do the flowers of the Roman nettle differ from those of the common stinging nettle?

11 Which animal group has members called midwife, spadefoot and firebellied?

12 Which is the odd one out: plum, date, cherry, apricot?

13 What kind of insect is a glow worm?

14 What is an inflorescence?

15 Chinese birds' nest soup is made from the dried saliva of a small swift: true or false?

16 What is the more familiar name of the goatsucker?

17 How many legs does a shrimp have?

18 Oxford ragwort is a native of Sicily, where it flourishes on the volcanic soils. Escaping from the botanic gardens in Oxford late in the 18th century, it spread slowly into the countryside at first, but at the beginning of the 20th century it began to spread very quickly. What facilitated its spread?

19 What insects have forms called duns and spinners?

20 Where is the Giant's Causeway?

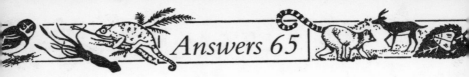

1 The study of the use of plants in folklore and religion

2 Long, slender, and pointed

3 Ducks

4 About 5000

5 A bird belonging to the cuckoo family (a good word for Scrabble enthusiasts)

6 South Africa

7 A climbing palm, whose stems may be over 150 m (500 ft) long

8 A fish

9 15th March to 15th June, inclusive

10 The flowers of the Roman nettle are in ball-shaped catkins, but those of the common stinging nettle are in slender, cylindrical catkins

11 Toads

12 The date: it is a single-seeded berry, but the others are stone fruits or drupes, with the seed enclosed in a woody case – the 'stone'

13 A beetle, although the wingless female looks more like a woodlouse

14 A flower cluster

15 True: the birds, found in Malaysia and Indonesia, make their cup-shaped nests almost entirely from saliva, which they stick to the walls of the caves in which they live

16 The nightjar

17 Ten

18 The railways: the tracks are similar to the volcanic soils in the plant's natural home, and winds created by the trains carried the seeds along

19 Mayflies: the duns are the rather dull and hairy sub-adults, while the spinners are fully mature and often quite shiny

20 On the coast of Northern Ireland. It is an ancient lava flow that formed thousands of hexagonal pillars as it cooled and contracted – in much the same way that hexagonal cracks appear in drying mud.

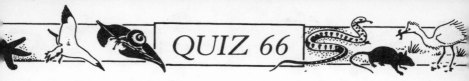

QUIZ 66

1 What is the red-billed quelea's claim to fame – or notoriety?

2 What is the main food of a lacewing?

3 What is the average life expectancy of a wild robin: 1 year, 5 years,, 10 years?

4 In what type of rock are most British caves formed?

5 What do pine, elder, and ivy have in common?

6 What do we call the moisture that accumulates on plants when the air cools down at night?

7 How many leaflets does a wood sorrel leaf have?

8 What is wrong with the following diary entry? 'My garden lupins looked decidedly unhappy one evening, and when I took a close look at them I saw that every leaf and stem was covered with plump aphids. I continued to watch, and under my lens I could see the aphids' jaws munching away at the leaves and rapidly reducing them to skeletons.'

9 Corymbs and umbels are both dome-shaped flower-heads, but what is the essential difference between them?

10 What is a godwit?

11 Name Australia's largest snake

12 To what major group or phylum of animals does the octopus belong?

13 In which county is the Lake District National Park?

14 How does the white bryony climb?

15 How does the black bryony climb?

16 The ratel is a carnivorous mammal of Africa and India: what is its alternative name?

17 What name is usually given to a fern leaf?

18 Which is the odd one out: cotton, silk, linen, sisal?

19 What kind of tree is the banyan?

20 How do crickets make their shrill calls or songs?

1 It is the most abundant wild bird in the world, with an estimated adult population of 1,500 million (it is also the most damaging bird, demolishing grain crops over a wide area of Africa every year)

2 Aphids

3 1 year

4 Limestone

5 They can all follow 'ground' to yield the names of other plants

6 Dew

7 Three

8 Aphids have no jaws: they suck sap through needle-like beaks

9 The individual flower stalks in a corymb are of different lengths and spring from different levels on the stem, but the flower stalks in an umbel all come from the same point on the stem, like the ribs of an umbrella

10 A wading bird

11 The taipan, which can reach lengths of about 4 m (13 ft)

12 The Mollusca or molluscs

13 Cumbria

14 With coiled, spring-like tendrils that cling to the neighbouring plants

15 By twining around the neighbouring plants

16 The honey badger

17 A frond

18 Silk: it comes from a caterpillar – the silkworm – and the others are all plant fibres

19 A fig tree

20 By rubbing their front wings together

QUIZ 67

1 Which is the odd one out: oyster, cockle, mussel, winkle?

2 What colour is blackthorn blossom?

3 What are dioecious plants?

4 Which of our native British trees supports the most insect species?

5 Which birds can be black, sooty, or roseate?

6 What sort of animal is a tarantula hawk?

7 Which is the most valuable fungus?

8 What is bioluminescence?

9 What animals are described as ovine?

10 What name is given to the communal display grounds where male black grouse display to attract females?

11 What is a Venus fly-trap?

12 Which fruit is used to make the alcoholic drink kirsch?

13 What have Avebury in Wiltshire, Callanish on the Isle of Lewis, and Castlerigg in Cumbria in common?

14 What kind of snake is most commonly used by snake charmers?

15 What is a quetzal?

16 What group of beetles have their jaws at the end of long, beak-like snouts?

17 What do captive raccoons often do with their food before eating it?

18 What common garden shrub is often called the butterfly bush because its flowers are so attractive to the insects?

19 What sort of flower is the heartsease?

20 What is Wookey Hole?

1 The winkle: it is a snail or gastropod and the others are bivalves

2 White

3 Those with male and female flowers on separate plants

4 The oak: over 300 insect species are known to feed on this tree

5 Terns

6 A large spider-hunting wasp

7 The truffle, a subterranean fungus. One ounce of the best quality French truffles can cost as much as £20

8 The production of light by living things, such as fireflies and glow-worms. The light is produced by a chemical reaction and is accompanied by almost no heat

9 Sheep

10 Leks

11 A carnivorous or insect-eating plant

12 The cherry

13 All have prehistoric stone circles

14 The cobra

15 A bird

16 Weevils

17 Dip it in water or wash it

18 The buddleia

19 A pansy

20 A cave in the Mendip Hills

1 What British butterfly shares its name with a fish?

2 What kind of animal features in the book *Watership Down*?

3 What is a mouflon?

4 What is special about the flight feathers of owls?

5 What bird was confined to the southeastern corner of Europe until the beginning of the 20th century but has now spread to almost every part of the continent?

6 What do hawk, chick, pond and duck have in common?

7 What is the more common name of the goat willow?

8 What kind of twigs are usually used for water divining?

9 What is metamorphosis?

10 What is a bonxie?

11 What would naturalists find of special interest at Welney and Slimbridge?

12 What familiar plant has varieties called Primo, Drumhead, and January King?

13 What are the dominant plants of the savanna?

14 How would you distinguish the flowers of coltsfoot and dandelions on sight?

15 Where would you find cowries and tellins?

16 How did the South American ovenbirds get their name?

17 What part of its host does an ectoparasite affect?

18 What kind of bird is a goosander?

19 From which plant do we get oregano?

20 Who wrote *My Family and other Animals*?

1 The grayling

2 Rabbits

3 A wild sheep

4 The leading edges of the flight feathers are very soft and make no noise in flight, so the owl can hear its prey but the prey cannot hear the owl

5 The collared dove

6 All can be followed by weed to yield the names of plants

7 The sallow or pussy willow

8 Hazel

9 The marked change in structure and appearance of an animal as it grows up. Familiar examples include the change from a caterpillar to a butterfly or a moth and the change from a tadpole to a frog or a toad

10 It is another name for the great skua (accept skua or bird)

11 Nature reserves or bird reserves – they are reserves of the Wildfowl and Wetlands Trust (accept wildfowl, waterfowl, ducks, or swans)

12 The cabbage

13 Grasses

14 Coltsfoot stalks are clothed with fleshy scales, but dandelion stalks are smooth

15 On the seashore – they are sea shells or molluscs

16 Because their domed nests of mud resemble old-fashioned bakers' ovens

17 The outside

18 A duck

19 Marjoram

20 Gerald Durrell

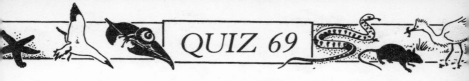

QUIZ 69

1 Which is the odd one out: kestrel, hobby, merlin or peregrine?

2 What plants were once known as scouring rushes or pewterworts and used to polish and clean milk pails and other metal objects?

3 Where, in 1985, did a ladybird appear together with a bumblebee, a wart-biter, a stag beetle, and a dragonfly?

4 What colour are the ripe fruits of the sea buckthorn?

5 What do we call the arm-over-arm movements that gibbons use to swing through the trees?

6 The codlin moth is a pest of which fruit tree?

7 What sort of animal is a vendace?

8 A specimen of *Encephalartos altensteinii* is believed to be the oldest glasshouse plant at Kew Gardens: what kind of plant is it?

9 Name the Norfolk naturalist who lived at Wheatfen Broad and became well-known for his 'nature spots' on BBC TV

10 Why is a sawfly so called?

11 Where in Britain would you find the grassy habitat known as machair?

12 What, in a flower, is the corolla?

13 What sort of webs do tarantulas spin?

14 What American mammal has been nicknamed the backstreet bandit?

15 Covert is the collective name for a flock of which waterbirds?

16 What have the following in common: tomato, deadly nightshade, aubergine, thorn-apple?

17 What is a tapir?

18 Name the world's deepest freshwater lake, which holds about a fifth of all the world's freshwater supplies

19 Where would you go to look for wild chamois?

20 What do we call an insect's breathing pores?

1 The hobby: it is a summer visitor to Britain and the others are all residents

2 Horsetails: they are covered with silica crystals which give them their rough texture

3 On British postage stamps

4 Orange

5 Brachiation

6 The apple tree

7 A fish

8 A cycad

9 Ted Ellis

10 Because the ovipositor or egg-laying apparatus of many species is like a tiny saw: it is used to cut slits in plants and to place the eggs in them

11 On the coast of Scotland, especially in the Hebrides and other western coasts; it is the strip of flat, sandy grassland just above high tide level

12 The whorl or whorls of petals

13 None: tarantulas are hunting spiders and do not spin webs to catch prey

14 The raccoon

15 Coots

16 They all belong to the Solanaceae or potato family (accept all belong to the same family)

17 A hoofed mammal related to horses and rhinoceroses

18 Lake Baikal in Russia: its maximum depth is about 1620 m (5320 ft – nearly a mile); it covers an area of about 31,500 km² (12,200 miles²), and it holds about 23,000 km³ of water

19 The Alps, Pyrenees, or other European mountains

20 Spiracles

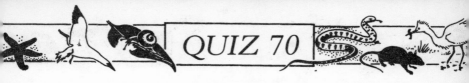

1 What is wrong with the following diary entry? 'Watching my garden pond one fine morning in March, I saw two frogs. One clung tightly to the other in the water and suddenly the larger one jerked violently and released a string of black eggs. The eggs kept coming until the string was about three metres long and thoroughly entangled in the water plants.'

2 Britain has two native oaks, the sessile oak and pedunculate oak: how do their acorns differ?

3 What bird appeared on the old farthing coin?

4 The red squirrel is larger than the grey squirrel: true or false?

5 What have geckoes and tree frogs in common?

6 Why are leaf-cutter ants often called parasol ants?

7 How many rhinoceros species are alive today?

8 In what kind of habitat would you search for jerboas?

9 What animal is the national emblem of South Africa?

10 Which birds can be crowned, booted, or golden?

11 What does a gardener mean when talking of short-day plants?

12 What is a mudskipper?

13 Which group of animals has the more species – the birds or the mammals?

14 Which animal has varieties called Burmese, Manx, and Silver Tabby?

15 What is a prickly pear?

16 What do we call the dust-like particles released by ferns and mushrooms?

17 What created most of the lakes in the northern hemisphere?

18 What is the principal food of an adult lamprey?

19 What colour is a skunk?

20 With what kind of animal was Joy Adamson associated?

1 Frogs lay their eggs in shapeless masses, not in strings (the animals described here are toads)

2 The acorns of the sessile oak have no stalks: those of the pedunculate oak have long stalks

3 The wren

4 False

5 They all have adhesive toe pads

6 Because the leaf fragments taken back to their nests are carried above their heads like parasols

7 Five: Indian, Javan, Sumatran, black and white

8 Desert habitat

9 The springbok or springbuck

10 Eagles

11 Plants that flower only when there is less than 12 hours of daylight. Garden chrysanthemums, for example, do not flower until autumn

12 A fish, living in tropical coastal waters, that can live out of water for a while and often scampers over the mud on its fins at low tide

13 The birds: about 9000 species compared with only 4500 mammals

14 The domestic cat

15 A kind of cactus

16 Spores

17 Ice or glaciers, sweeping over the land during the Ice Age. Some lakes were formed in hollows gouged out by the ice, and others developed where the glaciers dropped the material they were carrying and dammed up the valleys

18 Other fishes, especially their blood, which it obtains by rasping a hole in the skin with its teeth. It also consumes dead fish or carrion

19 Black and white

20 The lion

QUIZ 71

1 Name two birds found in Britain that have the word golden in their names

2 What does 'red sky at night' signify according to an old proverb?

3 What sort of animal is a Tasmanian devil?

4 How do eider ducks help us to keep warm at night?

5 What name, based on the colour of his coat, is given to the leader of a gorilla clan?

6 On which continent is the largest remaining area of rainforest to be found?

7 Where would you look for lugworms?

8 What do chameleons, cuttlefish, and plaice all have in common?

9 How many eyes does a scorpion have?

10 What is the main food of the white rhinoceros?

11 Which way do seagulls face when they land in windy weather?

12 What is common name of the bird *Passer domesticus*?

13 What does it mean if an animal or plant is said to be endemic to a particular region?

14 What colour are the ripe fruits of the buckthorn?

15 Why do howler monkeys howl?

16 What is an ocelot?

17 What, in the insect world, is a birdwing?

18 Why are ladybirds useful in the garden?

19 What have willow, wood, marsh and reed in common?

20 What name is usually given to a group of elephants?

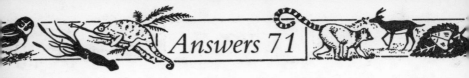

1 Any two from goldeneye, golden eagle, golden pheasant, golden plover or golden oriole

2 Shepherd's delight, or fine weather

3 A dog-like Australian marsupial

4 Because eiderdowns and duvets are often stuffed with their soft feathers

5 Silverback

6 South America

7 On the seashore, especially in the sand or mud

8 They can all change colour to match different backgrounds

9 Two

10 Grass

11 Into the wind, to prevent it from ruffling their feathers

12 The house sparrow

13 It is native to the region and not found elsewhere

14 Black

15 To establish their territories and warn other groups of howlers to keep away

16 A beautiful striped and spotted cat living in South and Central America

17 A butterfly, named for its extra-large wings

18 Because they eat aphids and other insect pests

19 They are all kinds of warblers

20 A herd

QUIZ 72

1 What is the common name of the large, colourful bird scientifically known as *Pavo cristatus*?

2 How did the kittiwake get its name?

3 Where was the cat first domesticated?

4 Name the series of TV programmes in which David Attenborough went in search of animals in various countries

5 How many teeth has a male narwhal?

6 What sort of animal is a tarsier?

7 What name is often given to the largest workers in an ant colony?

8 To which family of birds does the American roadrunner belong?

9 Name Britain's largest gull

10 What is unusual about the sloth's mode of life?

11 What is the fastest animal on four legs?

12 What have lime, pine, privet, and convolvulus in common?

13 Where might you find pineappleweed?

14 The nightingale always sings at night: true or false?

15 What colour is the male muslin ermine moth?

16 What sort of animal is a bonito?

17 How did the little plant called shepherd's purse get its name?

18 What is the proper name of the irritating little insects known as thunderbugs?

19 Which is the largest forest in England?

20 What do we call the line of seaweed and other debris left on the seashore when the tide goes out?

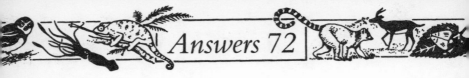

1 The peafowl (accept peacock)

2 From the sound of its call

3 In Egypt (accept Africa)

4 Zoo Quest

5 One – its solitary tusk

6 A large-eyed, nocturnal primate, related to the bushbaby and living in The Philippines and Indonesia (accept prosimian)

7 Soldiers, although they do not necessarily fight

8 The cuckoo family or Cuculidae

9 The great black-back or great black-backed gull

10 It does almost everything upside-down

11 The cheetah, which can run at about 112 kph (70 mph) for short distances

12 They are all the names of hawkmoths

13 On waste ground and trampled areas

14 False: it regularly sings by day as well as at night, but you can't hear it so well at night because all the other birds are singing

15 Brown

16 A fish

17 Because the flat seeds in the triangular capsules were thought to resemble coins in old-fashioned purses

18 Thrips

19 The Kielder Forest in Northumberland, covering about 61,000 hectares (150,000 acres) and forming part of the Border Forest Park

20 The strand line

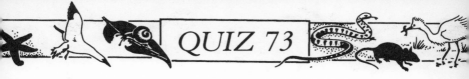

1 What kind of animal is a rorqual?

2 What is the fundamental difference between horns and antlers?

3 What is wrong with the following diary entry? 'The robins nesting in an old kettle in my hedge had reared a second brood and it was almost ready to fly. I could see the fluffy red breasts of the nestlings bobbing up and down as the birds struggled to heave themselves out of the nest.'

4 What sort of animal is a chuckwalla?

5 What is the older, inaccurate name of the dunnock?

6 What sort of animal is a cicada?

7 Black forms of many moths have spread through industrial areas in response to the blackening of tree trunks and other surfaces by smoke. By what name do we know this phenomenon?

8 In what kind of habitat would you expect to find the plant known as ling?

9 What kind of bird is represented by Horus, the bird-god of ancient Egypt?

10 Which is the odd one out: gannet, cormorant, tufted duck, dabchick?

11 Which fish's teeth are used as knives and razors by the Indians of South America?

12 What name is commonly applied to the yeti, the legendary man-like or ape-like creature alleged to inhabit the Himalayas?

13 What would you be eating if you sat down to a plate of ceps?

14 What is a sapsucker?

15 What colour are the flowers of Britain's two species of butterfly orchids?

16 How do the insects known as ant-lions trap their prey?

17 What kind of mammals belong to the group known as pinnipeds?

18 What is hoar frost?

19 What sort of creature is a woodworm?

20 What is a bower bird's bower?

1 A whale: the name is used for any member of the family Balaenopteridae, in which the throat region is deeply grooved

2 A horn consists of a horny sheath over a bony core, but an antler is solid bone. Horns are also unbranched and kept throughout life, but antlers are often branched and they are dropped and re-grown every year

3 Nestling robins do not have red breasts

4 An American lizard

5 The hedge sparrow

6 A sap-sucking bug famed for its piercing calls

7 Industrial melanism

8 Heathland or moorland. Ling is another name for heather (accept sandy places)

9 A falcon

10 The gannet: it dives into the water from the air but the other birds dive from the water surface

11 The piranha

12 The Abominable Snowman

13 Fungi. The cep, also known as the penny-bun fungus, is one of the best edible fungi (accept mushrooms and toadstools)

14 A North American woodpecker (accept bird)

15 White or cream

16 They excavate conical pits in sandy soil and lie in wait at the bottom to catch any insect that tumbles in

17 Seals and walruses

18 A deposit of fine ice crystals formed on plants and other surfaces when moisture condenses from the air at temperatures below freezing point

19 A beetle, although the name is really applicable only to the larva

20 A courtship and mating arena, built by the male to attract a mate and often decorated with flower petals and other bright objects

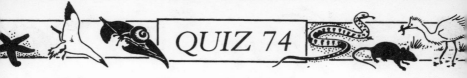

1 Which part of the world would you have to visit to look for wild hummingbirds?

2 Why has the red jungle fowl of India played an important part in feeding the world?

3 What is a tumblebug?

4 Which is the odd one out: ant, termite, cockroach, earwig?

5 How did the pasque flower get its name?

6 What is the alternative name for the king crab, which is not really a crab at all?

7 'One ... doesn't make a summer' according to the old proverb. What is the missing word?

8 What are Grasmere, Windermere, and Ullswater?

9 That is a jabiru?

10 What is unusual about pitcher plants?

11 What is the main food of the grass snake?

12 What birds or prey belong to the genus *Circus*?

13 What is a snail's operculum?

14 What is a fish's operculum?

15 Which insect group has species called foresters, footmen, and lackeys?

16 What is symbiosis?

17 What have hawthorn, meadowsweet and cinquefoil in common?

18 What sort of animal is a fer-de-lance?

19 Where is the Nullarbor Plain?

20 What does Nullarbor mean?

1 Almost any part of America, north, south, or central

2 Because it is the ancestor of the domestic chicken

3 A beetle: tumblebug is an American name given to those dung beetles that roll balls of animal dung around before burying them

4 Termite: it is the only one not native to the British Isles

5 From the French word Paques, meaning Easter, because the plant flowers at around Eastertime

6 Horseshoe crab: it is actually a marine arachnid

7 Swallow

8 Lakes in the English Lake District

9 A kind of stork

10 Their leaves form fluid-filled cups or pitchers, in which insects drown and are digested

11 Frogs

12 Harriers

13 The horny plate that covers the opening like a door when the snail retreats into its shell, but not present in all snails

14 The flap covering the gills on each side of the fish

15 The moths

16 It is a close association between two different kinds of animals or plants. It can cover any kind of association in which the partners live together, but is commonly restricted to those partnerships in which both partners gain some benefit. The partnership between a hermit crab and a sea anemone living on its shell is a familiar example

17 They all belong to the rose family or Rosaceae (accept all belong to the same family)

18 A venomous snake

19 Australia

20 No trees

1 What sort of animal is a moorish idol?

2 What kind of weather is best for catching moths?

3 What is the Jurassic Way?

4 What animals can be electric, moray, or conger?

5 In which country can you visit Yellowstone National Park?

6 What name is given to a young goat?

7 What is the proper name for the grass family?

8 What sort of insect is a chimney-sweeper?

9 What colour are the flowers of St John's-worts?

10 Which fruit is the odd one out: kumquat, loquat, mandarin, orange?

11 What is the better-known name of the cougar?

12 What is the main food of America's Everglades kite?

13 What is or was an ammonite?

14 What animals are associated with gossamer?

15 Which was the first of Britain's County Naturalists' Trusts to be formed?

16 What does the angler fish use as bait?

17 What have horse, cow and slug in common?

18 Which layer of the earth's atmosphere is causing concern among scientists because it appears to be getting thinner?

19 What sort of animal is an oxpecker?

20 What is the proper name for a snail's rasping tongue?

1 A fish commonly seen in tropical aquaria

2 Damp or humid weather with overcast skies

3 A long–distance footpath following the outcrop of Jurassic limestone from Stamford to Banbury. About 78 miles long, it was established by Northamptonshire County Council in 1994

4 Eels

5 The United States (accept America)

6 A kid

7 The Poaceae (accept Gramineae, which was the older name)

8 A moth, named for its sooty black colour

9 Yellow

10 The loquat: it belongs to the rose family and the others are all citrus fruits

11 The puma

12 Snails: it is sometimes called the snail kite

13 An extinct mollusc, related to the squids and octopuses, whose coiled shells are commonly found as fossils in clay and limestone rocks. There are many different species

14 Spiders: it is another name for spider silk

15 The Norfolk Naturalists' Trust, in 1926

16 A small flap of skin attached to a long, flexible fin-ray that hangs over the mouth like a fishing rod

17 All can be preceded by the word sea to give the name of another animal

18 The ozone layer

19 An African bird, named for its habit of perching on buffaloes and other large game animals and pecking off blood-sucking insects and ticks

20 The radula

1 What would you do with *Lactuca sativa*?

2 What do we call the tidal stretch of a river close to its mouth?

3 Is it the male or the female mosquito that bites us?

4 What do shrew, fern and creeper all have in common?

5 Where are the Galapagos Islands, on which Charles Darwin made many important observations to support of his theory of evolution?

6 What is a rhizome?

7 Who wrote the books on which the TV series All Creatures Great and Small was based?

8 Which is the odd one out: kingfisher, gannet, tern, osprey?

9 What sort of animal is a natterjack?

10 For what does a young dragonfly use its mask?

11 Which insect group has species called quakers, emeralds and carpets?

12 What is the more common name for the foulmart?

13 What is musophobia?

14 The sweet potato is a variety of potato in which much of the food is stored in the form of sugar instead of starch: true or false?

15 What is the connection between garden nasturtiums and watercress?

16 In botanical terms, what is a holdfast?

17 What colour are the flowers of the common mallow?

18 What are Ingleborough, Whernside and Pen-y-ghent?

19 What kind of creature is a sea–wasp?

20 What family of birds contains amazons, lories and macaws?

1 Eat it: it is lettuce

2 The estuary

3 The female: the male feeds only on nectar

4 All can be preceded by tree to give the names of plants or animals

5 In the Pacific Ocean

6 A horizontal stem, on or just below the surface of the ground and often packed with food reserves

7 James Herriot

8 The kingfisher: it fishes from a perch but the other birds all fly over the water as they search for fish

9 A toad

10 To catch prey: the mask is an extensible lower lip and it can be fired out at high speed to impale prey on the sharp claws at its tip

11 Moths

12 The polecat

13 A fear of mice

14 False: the sweet potato belongs to the convolvulus family and is not related to the potato, although the tubers often look alike

15 The scientific name of the watercress is *Nasturtium officinale*

16 It is the branched or sucker-like disc with which seaweeds cling to rocks

17 Pink or purple

18 Hills in North Yorkshire

19 A very poisonous jellyfish found in Australian waters

20 The parrot family (accept Psittacidae)

1 What kind of animal is a margay?

2 What is ordnance datum?

3 Which is the odd one out: rosemary, sage, mint, chervil?

4 If you met someone with the letters FZS after their name, what would be their profession or interest?

5 What colour is wild cherry blossom?

6 What bird is especially associated with Minsmere and Havergate on the Suffolk coast?

7 What is the collective name for a flock of quail?

8 How does a chameleon catch its prey?

9 What is wrong with the following diary entry? 'It had been a tiring journey along the banks of the Zambesi, but one more thrill awaited us as we approached the source of this mighty African river: there, lazing on the river bank, was a splendid tigress with two cubs

10 Which butterfly became extinct in Britain in 1979, but has now been successfully reintroduced to a few sites in southwest England?

11 What is the name of the long-distance footpath that runs from the Bristol Channel to Prestatyn on the coast of North Wales?

12 The word glaucous is often used in the descriptions of plants: what does it mean?

13 What trees belong to the widespread genus *Abies*?

14 What colour is a moth or other creature if it suffers from melanism?

15 *Ananas comosus* is a popular fruit. What is its common name?

16 What do kale, lavender and holly have in common?

17 What material forms the skeleton of a shark?

18 What insect order has groups called hawkers and darters?

19 Apart from being a variety of onion, what is Ailsa Craig?

20 John James Audubon was a famous American naturalist and painter, but what was his speciality, for which he particularly remembered?

1 A spotted cat from Central and South America

2 Sea level

3 Chervil: it belongs to the carrot family and the others are all members of the mint family

4 Zoology: it stands for Fellow of the Zoological Society of London (accept animals)

5 White

6 The avocet

7 A bevy

8 It shoots out its sticky tongue, which sticks firmly to the prey

9 Tigers do not live in Africa: they belong in Asia

10 The large blue

11 Offa's Dyke Path

12 Bluish green or with a bluish green waxy coating

13 Firs

14 Black or dark brown: melanin is a dark pigment and animals with an excess of it are very dark

15 Pineapple

16 They can all be preceded by sea to give the name of another plant

17 Cartilage

18 The Odonata or dragonflies

19 A rocky island in the Firth of Clyde a few mile south of Ayr

20 Bird painting

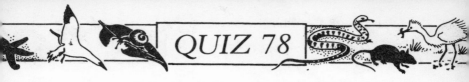

1 On the coast of which English county is Lulworth Cove, after which the Lulworth Skipper butterfly was named?

2 What sort of animal is a hawksbill?

3 Which short-legged dog is named after an English parson who developed the breed in the 18th century?

4 Which canal links London to Birmingham?

5 DNA is at the heart of the hereditary material that is passed from one generation to the next. What do the letters DNA stand for?

6 What do we call the excessive growth of algae that occurs from time to time, often as a result of pollution, and colours the water of lakes and other bodies of water?

7 What animals lived in huge colonies called towns, although these are much smaller now than they were in the past?

8 What is the nival zone on a mountain?

9 Which is the odd one out: chicory, dandelion, salsify, horseradish?

10 What is longshore drift?

11 What is an aspidistra?

12 What kind of animal is a basilisk?

13 Paddling is the collective name for what kinds of birds?

14 What would a naturalist find of interest at Braunton Burrows and Newborough Warren?

15 Which group of plants is the main source of sago?

16 What kind of mammal is a souslik?

17 What is an aquifer?

18 Where, on a plant, would you find a stipule?

19 What is the name given to the ancient art of chipping flints to make tools?

20 What is the biosphere?

1 Dorset

2 A turtle (accept reptile)

3 The Jack Russell

4 The Grand Union Canal

5 Deoxyribonucleic acid

6 An algal bloom

7 Prairie marmots, also called prairie dogs

8 The snow zone, which is covered with snow for all or much of the year

9 Horseradish: it belongs to the cabbage family and the others all belong to the composite or daisy family

10 The movement of sand and shingle along a beach, caused because waves usually come in at an angle but run straight back down the beach. Groynes may be installed to reduce the movement, and you can see how the sand or shingle piles up on the sides facing the incoming waves

11 An old-fashioned house plant with large dark green leaves that seemed to flourish in dark houses

12 A lizard

13 Ducks

14 Sand dunes: both areas, in North Devon and Anglesey respectively, are national nature reserves.

15 The palms, especially the sago palms of the genus *Metroxylon*. The sago is obtained from the pith in the centre of the sturdy stems

16 A ground-living squirrel

17 A layer of water-bearing rock

18 At the base of a leaf: it is an outgrowth from the leaf stalk and may be leafy or spiny

19 Flint-knapping

20 That part of the earth's surface (including the water and the air) that is inhabited by living things

1 What is an anemophilous plant?

2 When did the Palaeolithic (Pal-ee-oh-lithic) or Old Stone Age end in Britain: about 8000 years ago, about 80,000 years ago, or about 180,000 years ago?

3 What insects belong to the order Ephemeroptera (Eff-em-er-optera)?

4 Grasshopper eats grass, spider eats grasshopper, bird eats spider, cat eats bird. What name do we give to sequences of this kind?

5 What are blewits and boletes?

6 What bird is particularly associated with the Bass Rock in the Firth of Forth?

7 Why would a beachcomber be interested in MHW?

8 What ancient road runs from Devon to Lincoln?

9 Which is the odd one out: wheatear, mouse-ear, catsear, hare's-ear?

10 What starch-rich food is obtained from the roots of the cassava plant?

11 In the living world, what is a knot?

12 Shrews have poisonous bites: true or false?

13 What sort of insect is a firefly?

14 Which garden bird breaks snail shells by bashing them on stones?

15 By what common name do we know the genus *Aquilegia*, which contains many popular garden plants.

16 What is climax vegetation?

17 What river, immortalised in the paintings of John Constable, forms much of the boundary between Essex and Suffolk?

18 Which is the largest of the American cats?

19 What sort of animal is a char or charr?

20 How many legs has a daddy-long-legs?

1 A plant whose flowers are pollinated by the wind

2 About 8000 years ago

3 Mayflies

4 Food chains

5 Fungi or toadstools (accept mushrooms)

6 The gannet

7 Because MHW stands for mean highwater – the average level of high tide at any given place

8 The Fosse Way

9 The wheatear: it is a bird and the others are plants

10 Tapioca

11 A wading bird

12 True, although the poison is not likely to harm any human

13 A beetle

14 The song thrush

15 Columbines or granny-bonnets

16 The final stage in the development of the vegetation in any given area if it is not interfered with in any way. It is dependent upon the climate, and in most parts of the British Isles it would be forest

17 The Stour

18 The jaguar

19 A fish

20 Six – it is an insect, properly called a crane-fly

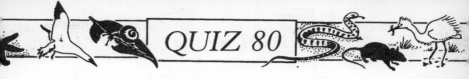

QUIZ 80

1 What is meant by the term F$_1$ hybrid, printed on many seed packets?

2 Where does a cauliflorous (col-ee-floor-us) tree bear its flowers?

3 What common geographical feature is sometimes called a knap?

4 What is oblong woodsia?

5 What goes through the Blisworth Tunnel in Northamptonshire?

6 Flowering plants are divided into two major groups – the monocotyledons and the dicotyledons: what is the essential difference between the two groups?

7 What kind of animal is a terrapin?

8 Fruticose lichens make up one of the major groups of these small plants: what does the word fruticose mean in this context?

9 Where might you find eel-grass growing?

10 Which is the odd one out: gazelle, gerenuk, gerbil, gnu?

11 What, in simple terms, is an exotic species?

12 What is dendroclimatology?

13 To what part of the body does the word dorsal apply?

14 What does it mean if a leaf is described as dentate?

15 Which region of the world do biologists refer to as the Palaearctic (Pal-ee-arctic) Realm?

16 What is the common name of plants in the genus *Euphorbia*?

17 What two colours are carried by most of the British burying beetles?

18 What kind of birds are scoters?

19 What does a biologist mean by biomass?

20 What is the pileus (pie-lee-us) of a mushroom?

1 The first generation of offspring produced by crossing or hybridising two different parental forms. Such hybrids often have unusual vigour, but they will not breed true in the next generation

2 On its trunk or major branches

3 A small hill

4 A fern

5 The Grand Union Canal

6 Monocotyledons have just one seed leaf (cotyledon) in their seeds, but dicotyledons have two seed leaves (monocotyledons generally have narrow leaves with parallel veins, while dicotyledons generally have broader leaves with a network of veins)

7 A freshwater turtle (accept tortoise or reptile)

8 Bushy

9 On the seashore, just below low-water mark. It is one of the few flowering plants able to grow in sea water

10 The gerbil: it is a rodent and the others are all antelopes

11 An alien or non-native species, living in an area to which it does not belong

12 The use of annual rings in trees to determine the climatic conditions at various times in the past

13 The back

14 It has a toothed margin

15 Europe and northern Asia (together with Africa north of the Sahara)

16 Spurges

17 Black and orange

18 Sea ducks

19 The total mass or weight of all the living organisms in a given area or habitat

20 The cap

1 Where do coprophilous organisms grow?

2 What are guenons and mangabeys?

3 Can you eat the leaves of the potato plant?

4 What animals go about in groups known as sleuths?

5 What is a bourn or bourne?

6 On what kinds of small plants would you find a calyptra?

7 Which insects have groups called bush, mole and cave?

8 What animals, commonly used to feed aquarium fish, are scientifically known as *Daphnia*?

9 What sort of animal is a cacomistle?

10 Which insects cause the distressing condition known as sheepstrike?

11 What is the field layer of a woodland?

12 What are larch roses?

13 What popular zoo animal has the scientific name *Pan troglodytes*?

14 Where does a geophytic plant spend the winter?

15 What does it mean if a plant is described as hispid?

16 What kind of animal is a tuatara?

17 The red food-colouring known as cochineal is obtained from the squashed bodies of cactus-feeding bugs: true or false?

18 What part of an animal is affected by endoparasites?

19 What do hyacinth, lily and plantain have in common?

20 How many legs does a harvestman have?

1 On dung

2 Monkeys

3 No – they are very poisonous, as are all green parts of the potato plant

4 Bears

5 A small stream, especially one that flows intermittently – like the many chalk streams that often flow only after the winter rains

6 Mosses: the calyptra is the little 'pixie hood' covering the unripe spore capsule

7 Crickets

8 Water fleas

9 A carnivorous mammal belonging to the raccoon family

10 Blow-flies: they lay their eggs in wounds on the sheep and the resulting maggots tunnel into the flesh and cause severe irritation. But under controlled conditions, maggots can actually be used to destroy diseased or infected flesh so that wounds can heal

11 The layer of herbaceous plants growing beneath the trees and shrubs

12 The young cones of the larch: they are bright pink and look like small roses

13 The chimpanzee

14 Under the ground, in the form of a bulb or some other resting stage that sends up new herbaceous shoots in the spring

15 It has short, bristly hairs (accept hairy or bristly)

16 A reptile from New Zealand, resembling a lizard but belonging to a much more ancient group and having no close relatives

17 True

18 The inside

19 All can be preceded by water to give the names of other plants

20 Eight

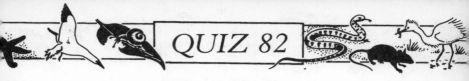

QUIZ 82

1 According to the Ordnance Survey, at what height does a hill become a mountain?

2 What have hen, flea and cow in common?

3 What, in the world of plants, are cryptogams?

4 What is dormancy?

5 What is entomophily?

6 What colour is a cardinal beetle?

7 If you buy a packet of cloves, what parts of the plant do you get?

8 Which group of plants are commonly described as the world's biggest grasses?

9 Where is Chesil Beach, Britain's most impressive bank of shingle?

10 What sort of animal is a sand mason?

11 What kind of plant is dulse?

12 In connection with the weather, what is nephology?

13 Name the world's largest species of penguin

14 What are King Alfred's cakes?

15 What kinds of birds belong to the family Laridae?

16 What part of the horseradish plant is used for making sauce?

17 What sort of mammal is a vicuna?

18 How many functional teeth does a mature garden snail have at any one time: about 50, about 1500, about 15,000 or about 50,000?

19 Which is the odd one out: cotton, linen, kapok?

20 What is an ephemeral plant?

1 2000 ft

2 All can be followed by 'bane' to give the name of a plant

3 Flowerless plants, such as ferns and mosses

4 A resting condition in plants and animals, in which the rate of metabolic activity is reduced to almost nil. Many seeds have to undergo a period of dormancy before they can germinate

5 Pollination by insects

6 Red

7 Unopened flower buds

8 Bamboos, although they are no longer placed in the grass family

9 Dorset

10 A marine worm that gets its name for its habit of building a tubular case with sand grains

11 A red seaweed

12 The study of clouds

13 The Emperor penguin, which reaches a height of about 110 cm (42 in)

14 Fungi, named for their rounded shape and dark brown or black colour – resembling burnt buns. The fungi grow on tree trunks and branches

15 Gulls

16 The root

17 A South American mammal belonging to the camel family. It lives high in the Andes and is famed for its fine wool

18 About 15,000

19 Linen: it comes from stem fibres but the others are fibres surrounding the seeds

20 A plant with a very short life cycle. Some desert plants live for no more than two or three weeks, sprouting from seed as soon as the short rainy season starts and dying when the ground dries up again – but not before flowering and scattering their own seeds

QUIZ 83

1 The roots of many plants form intimate connections with soil fungi, to the benefit of both organisms. What do we call such an association?

2 What animals make up the order Chiroptera?

3 What is the essential difference between a swamp and a marsh?

4 What are the principal flowers in the family Papaveraceae?

5 What does it mean if a plant or animal is described as indigenous?

6 Early in the 18th century, a Frenchman by the name of Bon made some gloves and stockings from spider silk: true or false?

7 What does a pedologist study?

8 What is heartwood?

9 Which part of the world do biologists refer to as the Nearctic Realm?

10 What is the common name of the animal scientifically known as *Panthera leo*?

11 What does it mean if an animal is described as gravid?

12 What would you do with *Pisum sativum*?

13 What sort of animals belong to the family Columbidae?

14 The rook is the largest member of the crow family: true or false?

15 What is the normal colour of speedwell flowers?

16 Which group of reptiles contains species called leathery and loggerhead?

17 What record is held by plants of the genus *Rafflesia*?

18 Name Britain's largest freshwater crustacean

19 In what sort of situation are you most likely to find ivy-leaved toadflax?

20 In what stage of its life cycle does the cabbage white butterfly pass the winter in Britain?

1 A mycorrhiza, which is an example of symbiosis

2 Bats

3 A swamp has standing water on it throughout the year but a marsh does not (although it may be flooded from time to time and the underlying soil remains waterlogged)

4 Poppies

5 It is native to the area in question, although not necessarily confined to it

6 True

7 Soils

8 The very hard timber from the centre of a tree trunk

9 North America

10 The lion

11 It means it is pregnant or full of eggs

12 Eat it: it is a garden pea

13 Pigeons and doves

14 False: the raven is the largest one

15 Blue

16 Turtles

17 They have the biggest individual flowers in the world – up to a metre (39 in) across – although the compound flower spikes of some arums are bigger

18 The crayfish

19 On old walls

20 The chrysalis stage or pupa

QUIZ 84

1 On which remote Scottish island is the world's largest gannetry?

2 What kinds of trees have the largest of all leaves?

3 What do the letters BSBI stand for?

4 Which common wayside tree, a favourite with wine-makers, has the scientific name *Sambucus nigra*?

5 Cinnamon is obtained from the crushed bark of a tree: true or false?

6 What, in the natural world, is a sport?

7 What do strawberry, tulip, bean and nettle all have in common?

8 What do thermophilous plants or animals enjoy?

9 How did the elephant hawkmoth get its name?

10 What does an ecologist mean by primary woodland?

11 What sort of animals belong to the family Ranidae?

12 A desert is a very dry area with little rainfall. Is it defined as an area with less than 5 cm, less than 25 cm, or less than 600 cm of rain per year?

13 Which TV naturalist wrote *The new Bird Table Book*?

14 What is the food-plant of the caterpillar of the meadow brown butterfly?

15 What sort of animal is an abalone?

16 Plant ecologists commonly talk about forbs: what are forbs?

17 What kinds of animals belong to the family Apidae?

18 How did the American mockingbird get its name?

19 In which county is Dartmoor National Park?

20 What is the main component of a house martin's nest?

1 St Kilda

2 The palms

3 Botanical Society of the British Isles

4 The elder

5 True

6 A freak, or an individual differing noticeably from the normal form of the species

7 All can be followed by tree to give the names of different plants

8 Warmth or sunshine

9 Because its caterpillar has a trunk–like snout

10 An area that has been forested since prehistoric times and has never been anything but woodland (accept natural woodland, although not all natural woodland is primary woodland)

11 Frogs

12 Less than 25 cm

13 Tony Soper

14 Grass of various kinds

15 A marine mollusc (accept sea snail but not bivalve)

16 Herbaceous plants, especially those growing in grassland, that are not grasses

17 Bees

18 From its ability to imitate or mock various other birds

19 Devon

20 Mud

1 What can you find at Horning, Hoveton and Hickling?

2 The BTCV is a voluntary organisation whose members carry out practical conservation work all over Britain. What do the letters BTCV stand for?

3 Apart from anchoring a plant in the ground, what vital function does a root perform?

4 Barbers used to hone their razors on bracket fungi: true or false?

5 What name is given to the fruits of the ash tree?

6 Why are some balsams known as touch-me-nots?

7 Where are the Gardens of the Rose?

8 Where is a firefly's lamp?

9 What animals belong to the family Leporidae?

10 What is a morel?

11 What name is given to soils containing about 30% clay, about 30% sand, and about 40% silt?

12 What are the principal plants in the family Juncaceae?

13 What sort of animal is an alewife?

14 What does a botanist mean by the lamina of a leaf?

15 What is a Clydesdale?

16 What sort of birds belong to family Paridae?

17 Where would you go to look for razorbills?

18 What colour are the flowers of the pheasant's-eye?

19 What name is given to the wind-sculptured pillars of rock seen on Dartmoor and in some other parts of south-west England?

20 If a plant is described as tomentose, what does it look like?

1 Lakes – they are three of the Norfolk Broads

2 British Trust for Conservation Volunteers

3 It absorbs water and mineral salts from the soil

4 True: some of these fungi are very tough and leathery and ideal for putting a final edge on a razor

5 Keys

6 Because the seed capsules explode if the plant is knocked and they throw out their seeds with sufficient force to sting your face if they hit you

7 St Albans (accept Hertfordshire)

8 Underneath its tail end

9 Rabbits and hares

10 An edible fungus (accept mushroom or toadstool)

11 Loams

12 Rushes

13 A fish

14 The blade

15 A breed of heavy horse or carthorse, originally developed in Scotland (accept horse)

16 Tits

17 Coastal cliffs (accept seashore or cliffs)

18 Red

19 Tors

20 Woolly, or covered with long hair

1 What part of the globe artichoke do we eat as a vegetable?

2 What part of the Jerusalem artichoke do we eat as a vegetable?

3 The slow-worm is one of Britain's three native species of lizards: name the other two

4 Where, on a plant, would you normally find the stomata?

5 Some termite species have blind workers whose heads are little more than reservoirs of glue, which is fired out through a nozzle at the front to ensnare enemies: true or false?

6 Poor man's ... is a country name for the scarlet pimpernel. What is the missing word?

7 What sort of animals are Charollais, Simmentals and Dexters?

8 How many wings does a flea have?

9 What do we call the bundles of indigestible matter that are regurgitated from time to time by owls and many other birds?

10 What, in the botanical world, are frogs, lizards and butterflies?

11 To what part of the body does the word caudal refer?

12 Rhizomania is a disease of which important crop in Britain?

13 The grubs of which common beetle are referred to as rookworms?

14 How does a plantigrade animal walk?

15 Which is the odd one out: orange, tomato, plum, gooseberry?

16 Where would you look for a gudgeon?

17 What sort of insect is the brown aeshna?

18 What sort of animal is a fennec?

19 What does a botanist, as opposed to a cook, mean by a herb?

20 What colour are the flowers of wild marjoram?

1 The young flowerheads or buds, especially the swollen bracts around the outside

2 The tubers

3 The viviparous lizard and the sand lizard (accept common lizard, which is another name for the viviparous lizard)

4 On the underside of the leaves

5 True

6 Weatherglass – a reference to the way in which the flowers close up in dull weather

7 Breeds of cattle

8 None

9 Pellets

10 Orchids

11 The tail

12 Sugar beet

13 The cockchafer – because rooks eat a lot of them on ploughed land

14 On the soles of its feet – like a bear or a human

15 The plum: it is a stone fruit and the others are berries

16 In lakes and streams: it is a freshwater fish

17 A dragonfly

18 A long-eared fox of the Sahara Desert

19 Any non-woody plant

20 Pink or purple

1 What shape are campanulate flowers?

2 What birds can be grey, ringed, or golden?

3 Whales spend almost all their lives at sea, coming ashore only to have their young: true or false?

4 Jack-by-the-... is one of several alternative names for garlic mustard. What is the missing word?

5 Britain has three native snake species: the adder, the grass snake – and what?

6 What kind of insect is sometimes known as the lousy watchman?

7 What sort of animal is a bulbul?

8 In the garden, what are HT's and floribundas?

9 Which European seabird has shown a dramatic increase in population in the last 200 years, possibly as a result of the increasing amounts of offal jettisoned by whaling boats and trawlers.

10 Which European tree can usually be recognised by the spiral bark pattern at the base of its trunk?

11 How can a fish's scales be used to estimate the age of the animal?

12 Where do the desert-dwelling honeypot ants store excess nectar for use during the dry season?

13 What colour are the fruits of the burnet rose?

14 Which magnificent bird is the national bird of India?

15 Eric Hosking was a renowned wildlife photographer, but what was his speciality?

16 What name is given to the cultivated variety of beech with purple leaves?

17 Which group of animals includes species called water, snow and field?

18 What is the essential characteristic of an entire leaf?

19 What popular confectionery is made from the latex of the chicle tree of Central Ameri

20 Under what name do we normally eat Norway lobsters?

1 Bell-shaped

2 Plovers

3 False: whales never come ashore

4 Hedge

5 The smooth snake

6 The dor beetle or dung beetle, which is often heavily infested with mites

7 A bird

8 Roses

9 The fulmar

10 The sweet chestnut

11 Because the scales grow with the fish and show annual growth rings like trees

12 In the swollen bodies of special worker ants, known as repletes

13 Black or purple

14 The peafowl (accept peacock, although this name really refers only to the male)

15 Bird photography

16 Copper beech

17 Voles

18 Its margin is completely smooth and untoothed

19 Chewing gum. The latex is also used in golf balls

20 Scampi

1 Who, in 1986, was quoted as saying 'To get the best results, you must talk to your vegetables'?

2 What kinds of insects have pollen baskets?

3 What trees can be Dutch, English, or Caucasian?

4 Iceland is fringed with extensive coral reefs: true or false?

5 What have kangaroo, mole and jerboa in common?

6 For what domesticated animal is Chillingham in Northumberland famous?

7 If a plant is described as procumbent, what does it do?

8 What sort of insect is a yellow sally?

9 What structural material forms the bulk of a plant and is probably the most abundant organic compound in the world?

10 Why do swallows fly off to Africa in the autumn?

11 What do we call a young whale?

12 What animals can be either geese or acorns?

13 What is the Old Man of Hoy?

14 Which is the longest of Britain's designated Long Distance Footpaths?

15 Which group of butterflies includes species called black, brown and white-letter?

16 What rare British carnivorous mammal has the scientific name *Lutra lutra*?

17 What colour are the flowers of fleabane?

18 Birds are the only animals with feathers: true or false?

19 What is the food-plant of caterpillar of the white admiral butterfly?

20 What is guano?

1 HRH The Prince of Wales

2 Bees

3 Elms

4 False: reef-building corals can live only in warm waters

5 All can be followed by rat to give the names of new animals

6 Cattle: Chillingham cattle are white and show many features of the ancestral aurochs

7 It sprawls over the ground

8 It is the angler's name for a stonefly

9 Cellulose

10 Because there are not enough flying insects for them to eat in the winter in Europe

11 A calf

12 Barnacles

13 A sea stack, or pillar of rock on the coast of Hoy in the Orkneys

14 The South-west Coast Path – about 515 miles round the coast from Minehead to Poole Harbour

15 The hairstreaks

16 The otter

17 Yellow

18 True

19 Honeysuckles

20 Dried bird excrement, especially that of sea birds, which accumulates in huge quantities in some areas and is used commercially as fertiliser

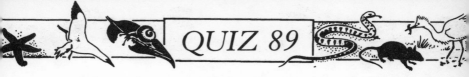

QUIZ 89

1 What group of plants contains species called hard, royal and shield?

2 Ducks, coots and moorhens all have webbed feet: true or false?

3 Scale insects cause severe damage to many crops, especially in the tropics: to what order of insects do they belong?

4 *Taxus baccata* is the scientific name of which British tree?

5 Which is the odd one out: hard rush, soft rush, Dutch rush, sand rush?

6 What are sedimentary rocks?

7 What kinds of animals belong to the family Cervidae?

8 Which is the tallest of all living animals?

9 What name is given to rain that falls through a polluted atmosphere and picks up compounds of sulphur and nitrogen?

10 What kinds of animals belong to the group known as annelids?

11 What is the difference between a martin and a marten?

12 What common shrub has the scientific name *Ulex europaeus*?

13 If you were unfortunate enough to be grabbed by a mugger, what kind of animal would you be battling with?

14 Name two British birds whose names contain the names of insects

15 What do we call a baby kangaroo?

16 What colour are the oystercatcher's legs?

17 What is the connection between Dunnet Head in Scotland and Lizard Point in Cornwall?

18 What is meant by the venation of a leaf or an insect wing?

19 What is the food of young stag beetles?

20 Which bird is sometimes referred to as the halcyon?

1 Ferns

2 False: ducks have webbed feet, but coots merely have lobes on their toes and moorhens have no webbing at all

3 The Hemiptera or bugs

4 The yew

5 Dutch rush: it is a horsetail and the others are true rushes

6 Rocks that were formed from sand and mud and other sediments deposited on the sea bed (and occasionally elsewhere)

7 Deer

8 The giraffe

9 Acid rain

10 Earthworms, bristleworms and leeches (accept worms)

11 A martin is a bird related to the swallows, while a marten is a mammal of the weasel family

12 Gorse

13 A crocodile

14 Grasshopper warbler and flycatcher – either pied or spotted

15 A joey

16 Pink

17 They are respectively the northern and southern extremities of mainland Britain

18 The arrangement of the veins

19 Dead wood: the beetles breed in dead tree stumps and other rotting timber

20 The kingfisher

QUIZ 90

1 There are no native woodpeckers in Ireland: true or false?

2 What group of plants contains species called pendulous, sand and bottle?

3 Which is the odd one out: tibia, femur, tarsus, antenna?

4 What colour are the ripe fruits of deadly nightshade?

5 What sort of bird is a teal?

6 How do toadstools of the genus *Boletus* differ from other umbrella-shaped toadstools?

7 What do stag, rhinoceros and tiger have in common apart from being mammals?

8 What kinds of insects possess halteres?

9 What is a gynandromorph (guy-nand-roe-morph)?

10 What era of geological time came between the Palaeozoic (Pal-ee-oh-zoh-ic) and the Cenozoic (Sen-oh-zoh-ic) eras?

11 What does it mean if an animal is described as having a good olfactory sense?

12 Which large mammals belong to the order Proboscidea?

13 What are nidicolous birds?

14 What would you expect to find in an herbarium?

15 Name the sea-snail with a conical shell that clings tightly to rocks on the seashore?

16 In the plant world, what is a pedicel?

17 What does a xylophagous animal eat?

18 What is the difference between the American animals known as chickarees and chickadees?

19 What is the common name of the plant whose scientific name is *Urtica dioica*?

20 What does an aphyllous plant lack?

1 True

2 Sedges

3 Antenna: the others are sections of legs

4 Black

5 A duck

6 *Boletus* species have a spongy layer under the cap, but the others have radiating gills

7 They are all kinds of beetles

8 Flies: the halteres are the pin-like 'balancers' derived from the hindwings

9 An abnormal animal in which some parts of the body have male features and others have female features. This condition is most common in insects and the division is sometimes right down the middle, producing an individual in which the two sides may have different colours

10 The Mesozoic Era

11 It has a good sense of smell

12 Elephants

13 Birds that hatch without feathers and stay in their nests for a good while

14 Dried plant specimens

15 The limpet

16 A flower stalk – strictly the stalk of an individual flower and not of a whole cluster

17 Wood

18 Chickarees are squirrels and chickadees are birds (of the tit family)

19 The stinging nettle

20 Leaves

1 What group of butterflies includes species called dark green, high brown and silver-washed?

2 Which well-known summer visitor has the scientific name *Cuculus canorus*?

3 When did the dinosaurs become extinct: about 7000 years ago, about 70,000 years ago, or about 70 million years ago?

4 In the insect world, what is an imago?

5 Three British birds have names beginning with 'long-tailed': name two of them

6 What is wrong with the following diary entry: 'We had been hacking our way through the rainforest for several days. It was virgin forest, previously untouched by man, and the undergrowth was so dense that it took us all day to travel a mile.'

7 What is taxonomy?

8 What is unusual about a peltate leaf?

9 For what purpose might a biologist use a pH meter?

10 Which is the odd one out: skate, ray, dogfish, hake?

11 What does a plant or animal look like if it is described as hirsute?

12 Poppy seeds can lie dormant in the soil for more than a hundred years without harm: true or false?

13 What kind of mammal is a linsang?

14 What is witches' butter?

15 By what common name do we know the angiosperms?

16 What family of mammals includes species called sambar, sika and white-tailed?

17 What trees can be oil, date, or sugar?

18 What is the function of a plant's tendrils?

19 Where would you expect to find halophytic plants growing?

20 What familiar fruit has the scientific name *Prunus persica*?

1 The fritillaries

2 The cuckoo

3 About 70 million years ago

4 An adult insect

5 Long-tailed tit, long-tailed duck, or long-tailed skua

6 Virgin rainforest has very little undergrowth – the canopy is so dense that few plants can grow beneath it

7 The science of describing and classifying living things

8 The stalk or petiole is attached to the centre, as in a nasturtium leaf

9 To measure acidity, especially the acidity of the soil

10 Hake: it is a bony fish and the others are cartilaginous fishes

11 It is hairy

12 True

13 A carnivorous mammal belonging to the mongoose family

14 A shiny, black, gelatinous fungus growing mainly on dead wood

15 The flowering plants

16 The deer family or Cervidae

17 Palm trees

18 They help the plant to climb

19 On the seashore or in a saltmarsh (accept salty ground)

20 The peach

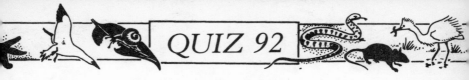

1 What does an entomologist hope to do by going 'sugaring'?

2 What brown seaweeds can be serrated, bladder, or channelled

3 What kinds of insects go in for slave-making?

4 What colour is the beak of a shelduck?

5 What is a cultivar?

6 What are cones, conches and cowries?

7 What do sessile leaves lack?

8 Where might you have trouble with blanketweed?

9 What name is usually given to the tail fins of a whale?

10 What is wrong with the following observation? 'It was a warm, damp night and the garden snails were mating everywhere – on the paths, on the plants and even on the walls. The males eagerly followed the females' slimy trails and mating took place after a brief flirtation and gentle touching of tentacles.'

11 Which is the odd one out: lime hawkmoth, pine hawkmoth, poplar hawkmoth, bedstraw hawkmoth?

12 To which family do the dahlia and chrysanthemum belong?

13 What, in the living world, is candle snuff?

14 If a plant is described as etiolated, what does it look like?

15 Which part of the world would you visit to watch animals in the Serengeti National Park?

16 What kinds of animals belong to the group called chelonians?

17 Which family of songbirds or perching birds is generally accepted to contain the most intelligent species?

18 What is a frogmouth?

19 To what mammals does the adjective cervine refer?

20 Evergreen trees never drop their leaves: true or false?

1 To catch moths: 'sugaring' involves painting tree trunks and other surface with a sugary mixture to attract the insects

2 The wracks

3 Ants: the workers of the slave-making species raid the nests of other species for pupae, and the ants emerging from the pupae work for their captors

4 Red

5 A cultivated variety of a plant

6 Sea shells or sea snails

7 Stalks

8 In a garden pond: blanketweed is a filamentous alga that often covers the surface and all the plants in a pond

9 Flukes

10 Garden snails are hermaphrodite animals and do not have separate males and females

11 The bedstraw hawkmoth: it is a scarce summer visitor to Britain and the others are resident moths

12 The daisy family or Asteraceae (accept Compositae, which is the old name for the family)

13 A fungus with ashy grey tips to its black branches

14 Pale and straggly: this is the typical appearance of plants that have been kept in the dark

15 East Africa. The park is in Tanzania

16 Turtles, tortoises and terrapins (accept any of these)

17 The crow family, or Corvidae

18 A bird related to the nightjars

19 Deer

20 False: evergreens replace their leaves quite regularly, but they do not drop them all at once

1 What sort of insect is a speckled yellow?

2 Which has the longer ears – a rabbit or a hare?

3 What is the common name of the bird scientifically known as *Tyto alba*?

4 Which is the odd one out: burnet rose, guelder rose, dog rose, field rose?

5 Where might you find thong-weed and bootlace weed?

6 To which order of mammals does the chinchilla belong?

7 How many leaves does a twayblade have?

8 Which group of marine animals includes beadlets, dahlias and snake-locks?

9 What does it mean if an insect is described as brachypterous?

10 Moas were giant birds that became extinct a few hundred years ago. Where did they live?

11 What do moths and penguins have in common?

12 What kind of animal is a flounder?

13 What material do honeybees use to build their combs?

14 Siege is the collective name sometimes used for a group of which large water birds?

15 What popular garden flower originated in Turkey and was originally called the Turk's cap?

16 What do horse, snake and scorpion have in common?

17 The kingcup is a common spring flower. By what other name do we know it?

18 What kind of mammal is an indri?

19 What is the proper name for the little suckers under the arms of starfishes and related animals?

20 What is zoophobia?

1 A moth

2 A hare

3 The barn owl

4 The guelder rose, which is not a true rose

5 On the seashore: they are seaweeds

6 The Rodentia, or rodents

7 Two

8 Sea anemones

9 It is short-winged

10 New Zealand

11 Both groups have species called emperors

12 A flatfish (accept fish)

13 Wax, produced in the bodies of the workers

14 Herons

15 The tulip

16 All can precede fly to give the names of new animals

17 Marsh marigold or May blobs

18 A lemur

19 Tube-feet

20 The fear of animals

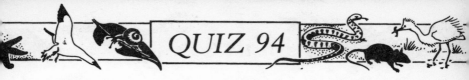

QUIZ 94

1 What common wild flower has the name *Lotus corniculatus*?

2 The male emperor moth can detect the scent of a female more than half a mile away: true or false?

3 What is or was an iguanodon?

4 Which insects belong to the order Dermaptera?

5 Where do epizoic animals live?

6 What are orange peel and golden spindles?

7 Which is the odd one out: sepal, carpel, anther, petiole?

8 What do omnivorous animals eat?

9 What, in the animal kingdom, is a crown of thorns?

10 Which animals belong to the family Equidae?

11 In which country can you visit the Yosemite National Park?

12 Where would you look for mosquito larvae?

13 What are the two main colours of the monarch butterfly?

14 Why were dung beetles deliberately released in Australia?

15 What name is given to a litter of piglets?

16 What would a botanist do with a vasculum?

17 What, on a duck, is the speculum?

18 What do pencil, incense and atlas have in common?

19 What is a barber fish?

20 What group of birds includes species called whooping, sarus and sandhill?

1 Bird's-foot trefoil

2 True

3 A dinosaur

4 Earwigs

5 On the bodies of other animals, although they are not parasitic. Barnacles living on the skin of a whale are good examples

6 Fungi

7 Petiole: it is a leaf stalk and the others are all parts of a flower

8 Both plant and animal matter (accept anything or everything)

9 A large starfish

10 Horses, zebras and asses (accept any or all of these)

11 The United States (accept America)

12 In stagnant water

13 Orange and black (accept red and black)

14 Because there were no native dung beetles capable of dealing with the huge amount of dung produced by the introduced sheep and cattle

15 A farrow

16 Put plant specimens in it: it is the botanist's traditional metal collecting box

17 The small patch of contrasting colour on the wing in certain ducks. It is often blue

18 They can all be followed by 'cedar' to give the names of trees

19 Any of various kinds of fish that remove parasites and damaged skin from larger species. Several kinds of wrasse do this and often 'set up shop' in a particular spot and wait for customers to arrive

20 Cranes

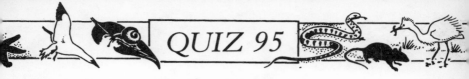

1 What sort of creature is a capercaillie?

2 What is the common name of the animal scientifically known as *Bufo bufo*?

3 What kinds of animals make up the family Felidae?

4 What, in the garden, are Peace, Albertine and Masquerade?

5 How many wings does a dragonfly have?

6 What kind of plant is cock's-foot?

7 On which English nature reserve has the Large Copper butterfly been maintained since the 1920s?

8 What is the shape of raven's tail when seen silhouetted against the sky in flight?

9 Heathers grow mainly on alkaline soils: true or false?

10 Which plant is traditionally used to treat the stings of stinging nettles?

11 What kinds of beetles belong to the family Coccinellidae?

12 What birds can be black-necked, red-necked, or great-crested?

13 Which large British mammal has the scientific name *Cervus elaphus*?

14 What strange name is sometimes given to a group or flock of crows?

15 What do entomophagous animals eat?

16 What is a hibernaculum?

17 Where would you search for hydrophytic plants?

18 What are grunts and gobies?

19 What name is given to the male moose or elk?

20 What sort of animal is a honeycreeper?

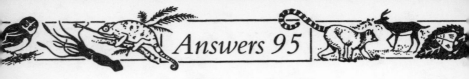

1 A large gamebird (accept bird)

2 The common toad

3 Cats

4 Roses

5 Four

6 A grass

7 Woodwalton Fen

8 Wedge-shaped or diamond-shaped

9 False: most heathers require acidic soils, although some cultivated forms can survive on alkaline soils

10 The dock

11 Ladybirds

12 Grebes

13 The red deer

14 A murder

15 Insects

16 A hibernation chamber in which hibernating animals go to sleep

17 In or around water: the name means 'water-loving'

18 Fish

19 A bull

20 A bird

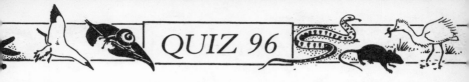

QUIZ 96

1 What flowers are called peggles or paigles in some areas, especially in East Anglia?

2 A football-sized puffball may contain more than 1,000,000,000,000 spores: true or false?

3 Which British mammal has the scientific name *Dama dama*?

4 What is a polymorphic animal or plant?

5 What do eyebright, mistletoe and yellow rattle have in common?

6 Which birds belong to the family Anatidae?

7 What familiar flower has the scientific name *Bellis perennis*?

8 What are hexapods?

9 Which animal has races known as Siberian, Bengal and Caspian?

10 What do click, screech and blister have in common in the insect world?

11 What tree would you expect to grow from a prune stone?

12 Which continent is home to the hippopotamus?

13 To which order of insects do the aphids belong?

14 Which popular bird is associated with Lundy Island?

15 What sort of animal is a cuscus?

16 Which group of trees makes up the bulk of Australia's forests?

17 Which group of birds includes species called crested, blue and great?

18 What did Cornish people once refer to as the Cornish Alps?

19 What record is held by the South Georgia Pipit?

20 What is an inchworm?

1 Cowslips and also oxlips

2 True

3 The fallow deer

4 A species that exists in two or more different forms

5 They are all partial parasites (or hemi-parasites): although they contain chlorophyll and can carry out photosynthesis, they get water and minerals from their hosts

6 Ducks, geese and swans (accept any or all of these)

7 The daisy

8 Hexapods, meaning six-legged, is another name for insects

9 The tiger

10 They are all beetles

11 A plum tree

12 Africa

13 The Hemiptera (accept bugs)

14 The puffin

15 A marsupial belonging to the phalanger group, living in Australia and New Guinea

16 The eucalyptus trees or gum trees

17 The tits

18 The spoil heaps from the tin mines

19 It is the most southerly of all song birds or passerines

20 A caterpillar: it is an American name for a looper caterpillar

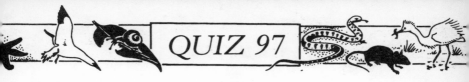

QUIZ 97

1 What sort of creature is a horntail?

2 What are goannas, iguanas and anoles?

3 In what stage of their life history do British grasshoppers pass the winter?

4 Jack-go-to-bed-at-noon is a country name for which common plant?

5 Where might you find a phantom larva?

6 What collective name is given to all the plants and animals of a given area or a given period of geological time?

7 What colour are the flowers of the biting stonecrop?

8 What is unusual about the fiddler crabs of tropical shores?

9 What sort of animals are caught in Longworth traps?

10 What flavour would salad burnet leaves impart to your drinks and salads?

11 Which group of birds includes species called wood, crested and shore?

12 What sort of animal is a gurnard?

13 Which small mammals have red-tipped teeth?

14 How did jewelweed, a common waterside plant, get its name?

15 What is wrong with the following diary entry? 'Spring was in the air as I walked through the hazel copse. Yellow catkins festooned the branches, and the buzzing of the early bumble bees filled the air as the insects eagerly gathered nectar and pollen from the catkins.'

16 What sort of plant is sorghum?

17 Starfishes and sea urchins belong to the group of animals known as echinoderms. What does this name mean?

18 What are greylags and pinkfoots?

19 Which part of the world would you visit to look for arrow-poison frogs?

20 Do young fleas suck blood?

1 A large sawfly, also known as a woodwasp. It gets its name for the fearsome-looking spike at the rear of the female, but this is just an egg-layer and the insect is quite harmless

2 Lizards

3 The egg stage

4 The goat's-beard, whose flowers usually open in the morning sunshine and close up about mid-day

5 In a pond: it is the larva of a small midge and it got its name because its body is almost completely transparent

6 The biota

7 Yellow

8 The male crab has one of his claws greatly enlarged: it is sometimes bigger than his body and he uses it to signal to the females

9 Small mammals, such as mice, voles and shrews

10 Cucumber

11 Larks

12 A fish

13 Shrews, although not all species actually have red tips

14 Because the leaves give out droplets of water that glisten in the sunshine

15 Hazel catkins are pollinated by the wind and are not visited by bees

16 A cereal (accept grass or grain)

17 Spiny-skinned

18 Geese

19 South America

20 No: they feed on debris in the nests of their hosts, but they do need blood and they get it 'second hand' by eating the droppings of the adult fleas

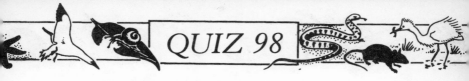

QUIZ 98

1. Who wrote *King Solomon's Ring*?

2. Where would you find clints and grikes?

3. What bird nested in the British Isles for the first time in 1967, when a pair settled on the island of Fetlar in the Shetland Isles?

4. Caper spurge is said to repel which small mammal?

5. Which organisation is the largest private land-owner in Britain?

6. What sort of fruit is a mirabelle?

7. What is the name of the wooden or concrete structures built at right angles to the shore to stop the drifting of sand and shingle?

8. Which is the odd one out: wheat, oats, barley, rye?

9. Where would you be if you were watching aardvarks in the wild?

10. What are the two principal colours of the English swallowtail butterfly?

11. What is a rat-tailed maggot?

12. What kinds of birds are noddies?

13. Which is the only snake regularly found north of the Arctic Circle?

14. What do whortleberry, blaeberry, blueberry and bilberry have in common?

15. To which family of birds does the mynah belong?

16. What sort of animals belong to the family Lacertidae?

17. What name is given to a young goose?

18. What animals have species called spiny, house and yellow-necked?

19. Lamp-shells are better known as fossils than as living animals. What is their more familiar name?

20. On a map, what are isotherms?

1 Konrad Lorenz

2 On a limestone pavement: clints are the limestone slabs and grikes are the grooves or fissures between them

3 The snowy owl

4 The mole

5 The National Trust, which owns nearly 600,000 acres of the most beautiful countryside in Britain

6 A small plum

7 Groynes

8 Oats: it bears its grain in open sprays and the others form tight ears

9 Africa

10 Yellow and black

11 The aquatic larva of a hover-fly – named for its slender 'tail', which is actually a sort of snorkel tube enabling it to draw air from the surface

12 Terns living in tropical regions

13 The adder

14 They are all names for the same plant

15 The starling family (accept Sturnidae)

16 Lizards

17 A gosling

18 Mice

19 Brachiopods

20 Lines joining places with the same average temperatures

1 What colour are the flowers of the meadow clary?

2 Name the famous fenland nature reserve between Cambridge and Ely.

3 What will happen, according to an ancient belief, if it rains on St Swithin's Day?

4 When is St Swithin's day?

5 What insects belong to the family Syrphidae?

6 What have sand, wound, milk and rag in common?

7 How can hanging a piece of seaweed outside your door help you to forecast the weather?

8 What do gypsies call hotchiwitchi?

9 What do we call the little cushions from which cactus spines arise?

10 Which was Britain's first National Nature Reserve?

11 After whom were Australia's magnificent *Banksia* flowers named?

12 What are lynchets?

13 What is a garganey?

14 What beetle was sacred to the Egyptians and appears on many ancient buildings and monuments?

15 The World Wide Fund for Nature is a major international conservation organisation, but what was it called originally?

16 What is boulder clay?

17 What is unusual about a chameleon's eyes?

18 Which is the odd one out: clouded yellow, red admiral, yellow underwing, meadow brown?

19 What is a pawpaw?

20 Where would you find a buckie?

1 Bright blue

2 Wicken Fen

3 It will rain for another 40 days

4 15th July

5 Hover-flies

6 All can be followed by wort to give the names of plants

7 Because the seaweed absorbs moisture and becomes limp when the air becomes damp, and this is most likely to happen when it is going to rain

8 Hedgehogs

9 Areoles

10 Beinn Eighe in the Scottish Highlands, set up in 1951

11 Sir Joseph Banks, a naturalist who sailed with Captain Cook

12 Small ridges or terraces on hillsides, formed by ploughing in prehistoric times

13 A duck

14 The scarab

15 The World Wildlife Fund

16 The mixture of clay, rocks and stones picked up by the ice-age glaciers and then dropped when they melted. Often many feet thick, it covers large areas of Britain and other parts of northern Europe

17 They move independently and can look in two completely different directions at the same time

18 The yellow underwing: it is a moth and the others are butterflies

19 A tropical fruit

20 On the seashore: it is another name for the whelk

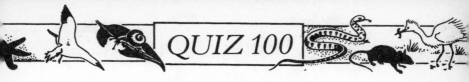

1 What kind of logs did Good King Wenceslas ask to be brought to him?

2 Turkeys come from Turkey: true or false?

3 What tree is traditionally used as a Christmas tree?

4 Name three of Santa's traditional reindeer.

5 One of the Three Wise Men brought resin from the tree *Boswellia carterii*. What is its more familiar name?

6 What have 25th December, *Phoenix dactylifera*, and 1st April in common?

7 What is the basic shape of all snowflakes?

8 Where might you find a cow, a bean and a goose appearing together at Christmas time?

9 What would you do with a mixture containing *Salvia officinalis* and *Allium cepa*?

10 What did Little Jack Horner pull out of his Christmas pie?

11 Tangerines, also known as mandarins, are popular at Christmas. They first arrived in Europe in the 18th century – from where?

12 What is the common name of the plant *Schlumbergera truncatus* (also called *Zygocactus truncatus*) that commonly flowers at Christmas?

13 What was Rudolph's shining glory?

14 According to a popular Christmas song, what does the singer receive on the seventh day of Christmas?

15 How does *Erithacus rubecula* come into most of our homes at Christmas?

16 Which of the following are true nuts: cobnut, almond, Brazil nut, chestnut, walnut?

17 What is the name of the plant, often given as a Christmas present, that has brilliant red bracts around its flowers?

18 *The holly and the ...* is a popular Christmas carol. What is the missing word?

19 Marzipan is made from sugar, egg-whites and what?

20 What might you steal under *Viscum album*?

1 Pine logs

2 False: they come from North America

3 The spruce

4 Any three from: Blitzen, Comet, Cupid, Dancer, Dasher, Donner, Prancer, Vixen

5 Frankincense

6 They are all dates

7 Hexagonal or six-sided

8 In the pantomime Jack and the Beanstalk

9 Shove it in your Christmas turkey or chicken: it is sage and onion stuffing

10 A plum

11 China and south-east Asia

12 Christmas cactus

13 His nose

14 Seven swans a'swimming

15 As a picture on a Christmas card: *Erithacus rubecula* is the scientific name of the robin

16 The cobnut and the chestnut are true nuts: they are complete fruits, but the others are all only parts of fruits

17 Pointsettia

18 Ivy

19 Ground almonds

20 A kiss: *Viscum album* is mistletoe

The following 100 questions can be used as tie-breaks – one for each of the main quizzes – or can be played on their own for fun. Questions printed in capitals are anagrams. Many of the others are in the form of 'brain-teasers', and if you interpret the clues in the right way you will come up with the names of plants and animals. Here is an example:

Clue: Rough up the fruit

Answer: Raspberry (rasp berry)

Most of the answers are the names of European plants or animals

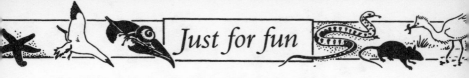

Just for fun

1 JOIN A MATHS UNION TO FIND THIS TREE

2 Who killed Cock Robin in the nursery rhyme?

3 REAP CORN WITH FEELING FOR THIS BIRD

4 What kind of animal is Kevin, Roland Rat's TV friend?

5 A second helping of chicken perhaps

6 Aerial prank

7 SORT OUT HAT TROUBLE TO FIND THIS BIRD

8 Cox of the Cambridge boat perhaps

9 HIS OLD GRAMMAR WILL REVEAL THIS WATER-LOVING FLOWER

10 What sportsmen are interested in birdies?

11 RED WOMAN BOWS TO FIND THESE BUTTERFLIES

12 Canterbury Cathedral perhaps

13 TURN GREED SOUR FOR THIS BIRD

14 Perm the sheep perhaps

15 DOES THIS BUTTERFLY HACK TRAIL BREAKS?

16 What sort of animal was Moby Dick?

17 High-class butchers would not use these

18 WHAT BUTTERFLY DULY COOED WELL?

19 Tease the unhealthy

20 A SIKH SEED LORRY OVERTURNED IN THIS NATIONAL PARK

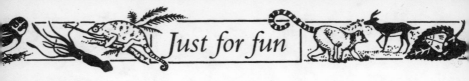

Just for fun

1 Mountain Ash
2 The sparrow
3 Peregrine falcon
4 A gerbil
5 Moorhen
6 Skylark
7 Bluethroat
8 Small blue
9 Marsh marigold
10 Golfers
11 Meadow browns
12 Kentish glory
13 Red grouse
14 Curlew
15 Black hairstreak
16 A sperm whale
17 Common cleavers
18 Clouded yellow
19 Tormentil
20 Yorkshire Dales

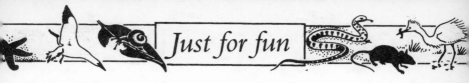

Just for fun

21 Geoff Capes was one

22 ROB HERBERT TO GET THIS PLANT

23 Might take to the air one day

24 Which bit of a newt do the witches of *Macbeth* stir into their cauldron?

25 GO ON A BOW TRAIN TOUR TO SEE THIS FISH

26 Send your account to the fruit

27 What was the name of Dr Doolittle's double-headed llama?

28 KIND HEARTS PICK C-BEETLES FOR THIS FISH

29 Moisten the salad

30 STUN THE CHORES TO GET THIS TREE

31 Graham Gooch was one

32 PEEL CALM REPRINTS TO FIND THIS COLOURFUL FLOWER

33 Study the flags perhaps

34 A short spell of duty

35 THEN NOD PLAYS FOR A SMALL HORSE

36 A WIND SOON BLOWS AROUND IN THIS NATIONAL PARK

37 Which animal sold the wedding ring to the owl and the pussy cat in Edward Lear's poem The Owl and the Pussycat?

38 Scared naval officer

39 According to the nursery rhyme, what were the only things that would grow on 'my little nut tree'?

40 WOULD THIS LITTLE RODENT HAVE OUR STEMS?

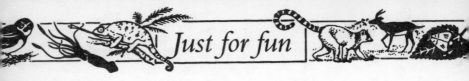

Just for fun

21 Large copper

22 Herb Robert

23 Mayfly

24 Eye

25 Rainbow trout

26 Bilberry

27 A pushmi-pullyu

28 Three-spined stickleback

29 Watercress

30 Horse chestnut

31 Essex skipper

32 Scarlet pimpernel

33 Reed bunting

34 Little stint

35 Shetland pony

36 Snowdonia

37 A pig

38 White admiral

39 A silver nutmeg and a golden pear

40 Harvest mouse

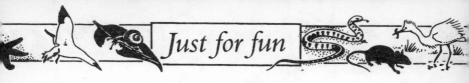

Just for fun

41 What bird is used at all major cricket matches?

42 Could this be an uplifting account?

43 SILLY PAT PLUCKED BUD FOR THIS WEIRD ANIMAL

44 Who wrote about Mrs Tiggywinkle?

45 THIS NATURALIST MAY BE AVIDLY BLAMED – FOR MAKING GOOD TV PROGRAMMES PERHAPS

46 A 'PINTA' FRENCH ALE FOR THIS BIG ANIMAL PLEASE

47 What flowers surround your mouth?

48 Which book tells us that 'All animals are equal, but some animals are more equal than others'?

49 PAT WENT LAME AND FOUND THIS AMPHIBIAN

50 Could this little animal really be Friar Tuck?

51 Does this butterfly have old-fashioned curls?

52 IS THIS IS BIRD REALLY CLEAR OF PREENING?

53 What animal wallowed in glorious mud according to a famous song by Flanders and Swan?

54 BOIL DRIFTER'S FOOT AND YOU'LL FIND THIS LITTLE FLOWER

55 Who wrote Animal Farm?

56 COULD THIS MARINE CREATURE BE RESPONSIBLE FOR A PURE WOMAN'S OUTRAGE?

57 What famous fictional bear lives in Nutwood?

58 MOTORISTS MIGHT FIND FREE STOPPING IN THIS SYLVAN SETTING

59 YOU'LL HAVE TO PLOD OVER GLEN TO FIND THIS BIRD

60 With which London animals do you associate the artist Edwin Landseer?

Just for fun

41 A roller

42 Crane's-bill

43 Duckbilled platypus

44 Beatrix Potter

45 David Bellamy

46 African elephant

47 Tulips

48 *Animal Farm*

49 Palmate newt

50 Chipmunk

51 Ringlet

52 Peregrine falcon

53 The hippopotamus

54 Bird's foot trefoil

55 George Orwell

56 Portuguese man 'o war

57 Rupert

58 Epping Forest

59 Golden plover

60 The Lions in Trafalgar Square: Landseer designed them

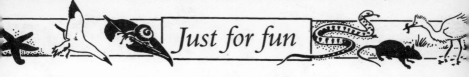

61 PERHAPS THIS NATURALIST AIDED ROUGH BAT ON TV

62 What instruments play the part of the wolf in *Peter and the Wolf* by Prokofiev?

63 HELP SKIN VOTER TO FIND THIS BIRD

64 From where did Paddington Bear originally come?

65 A LONGER DOWEL FOR THIS BIRD PLEASE

66 Would this bird prevail in the discussion?

67 PACK HUMBLE HAW FOR THIS MARINE ANIMAL

68 WOULD ANY CROW SQUINT TO FIND THIS LITTLE PLANT?

69 With what kinds of animals do you associate the painter George Stubbs?

70 What kind of animal was the 'very friendly' TV puppet called parsley?

71 DID BORIS'S TRENCH UNEARTH THIS DULL FLOWER?

72 To what did Nellie the Elephant say goodbye when she packed her trunk?

73 In which musical do we hear about the exploits of Mr Mistoffolees?

74 ARE THESE GARDEN FLOWERS ALWAYS IN NEED OF MEASURING?

75 Who wrote *The Thieving Magpie*?

76 WERE THERE ONCE CRAB BONES IN THIS NATIONAL PARK?

77 Tie up the troublesome plant

78 FILL IN HARROW BY RIGHT TO FIND THIS BUTTERFLY

79 What sort of animal is TV's Kermit?

80 Girl consumed seabird perhaps

Just for fun

61 David Attenborough

62 Three horns

63 Kentish plover

64 Darkest Peru

65 Long eared owl

66 Whinchat

67 Humpback whale

68 Squinancywort

69 Horses

70 A lion

71 Bird's nest orchid

72 The circus

73 Cats

74 Geraniums

75 Rossini

76 Brecon Beacons

77 Bindweed

78 High brown fritillary

79 A frog

80 Roseate tern

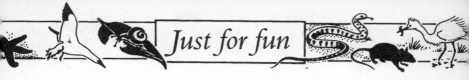

81 Which bit of a frog do the witches of Macbeth stir into their cauldron?

82 How many dogs run in an English Greyhound Derby final?

83 'Hail to thee, blithe spirit! Bird thou never wert, that from heaven, or near it, pourest thy full heart...' At what bird was the poet Shelley aiming these words?

84 FLANDERS IS AN UNUSUAL SEAL SANCTUARY IN THE NORTH SEA

85 What animal is the symbol of the American Republican Party?

86 What is the name of Rupert's elephant chum?

87 WHOSE NEAT OLD BELT PROVIDES THIS MARINE CREATURE?

88 Which famous stories featured the roc – a bird reputed to be strong enough to lift an elephant?

89 How many blackbirds were baked in the pie?

90 Name TV's first Blue Peter dog

91 Angry William

92 PADDY ATE NIL AND FOUND A BUTTERFLY

93 Peddle the marijuana

94 Who wrote the Flower Fairies poems?

95 Which President of the United States had a wife known as Ladybird?

96 IS BLUE CAMEL BY WATER REALLY A BUTTERFLY?

97 Fuels the tempest perhaps

98 PARE THE LISTS TO FIND THIS COMMON PLANT

99 What sort of Italian dish would you be eating if you were served with 'little worms'?

100 Hit Christmas – with a bat perhaps!

81 A toe

82 Six

83 The skylark

84 Farne Islands

85 The ass

86 Edward Trunk

87 Bottlenosed whale

88 TheArabian Nights

89 24

90 Petra

91 Crossbill

92 Painted lady

93 Hawkweed

94 Cicely M. Barker

95 Lyndon Johnson

96 Camberwell beauty

97 Storm petrel

98 Spear thistle

99 Vermicelli

100 Noctule